SIMPLICIUS
On Aristotle's
"On the Heavens 1.10-12"

Translated by
R.J. Hankinson

Cornell University Press

Ithaca, New York

Preface © 2006 by Richard Sorabji
Translation and Notes © 2006 by R.J. Hankinson

All rights reserved. Except for brief
quotations in a review, this book, or parts
thereof, must not be reproduced in any form
without permission in writing from the publisher.
For information address Cornell University Press,
Sage House, 512 East State Street, Ithaca, New York 14850.

First published 2006 by Cornell University Press.

ISBN 978-0-8014-4216-2
0-8014-4216-8

Acknowledgments

The present translations have been made possible by generous and imaginative funding from the following sources: the National Endowment for the Humanities, Division of Research Programs, an independent federal agency of the USA; the Leverhulme Trust; the British Academy; the Jowett Copyright Trustees; the Royal Society (UK); Centro Internazionale A. Beltrame di Storia dello Spazio e del Tempo (Padua); Mario Mignucci; Liverpool University; the Leventis Foundation; the Arts and Humanities Research Board of the British Academy; the Esmée Fairbairn Charitable Trust; the Henry Brown Trust; Mr and Mrs N. Egon; the Netherlands Organisation for Scientific Research (NWO/GW); Dr Victoria Solomonides, the Cultural Attaché of the Greek Embassy in London. The editor wishes to thank Guy Guldentops, Richard McKirahan, and Henry Mendell for their comments, and John Bowin, Michael Griffin, and Inna Kupreeva for preparing the volume for press, and Deborah Blake who has been Duckworth's editor for all volumes in the series since the beginning.

Printed and bound in Great Britain

Librarians: Library of Congress Cataloging-in-
Publication Data are available.

SIMPLICIUS

On Aristotle's

"On the Heavens 1.10-12"

Contents

Preface	vii
Textual Emendations	ix
Translation	3
Notes	83
Select Bibliography	117
English-Greek Glossary	121
Greek-English Index	125
Subject Index	131

Preface

Richard Sorabji

In these three chapters, Aristotle argues that the universe is ungenerated and indestructible. Whereas in Philoponus' *Against Proclus* we see a battle royal between a Christian (Philoponus) and a Platonist on the subject of the world's eternity, here we see a battle between Philoponus' Platonist rival, Simplicius, the Neoplatonist of the sixth century AD, and the Aristotelian, Alexander, who wrote around 200.

Commenting at 297,1-301,28, Simplicius quotes the lost commentary of Alexander on Aristotle's *On the Heavens*, just as Philoponus does in *Against Proclus on the Eternity of the World*, 212,14-222,17. But whereas Philoponus takes the side of Alexander, arguing that Plato's *Timaeus* gives a beginning to the universe, Simplicius takes the Platonist side, which had in *Against Proclus* been represented by Taurus, Porphyry, and Proclus, and denies that Plato intended a beginning. The origin (*arkhê*) to which Plato refers is, according to Simplicius, not a temporal origin, but the divine cause that produces the world without beginning, 299,22-3. Alexander and Aristotle recognise that the world is eternal, but whereas Alexander rejects God as its cause, Simplicius is convinced by his teacher Ammonius that Aristotle did so recognise God, 301,4-7; cf. 271,18-21.

Philoponus, in *Against Proclus* 242,15-22, infers from Proclus' account that Plato's God would have to override the natural destructibility of the universe, in order to keep it in being, and this is strongly suggested by Plato himself at *Timaeus* 41A-B. But Simplicius, addressing this view, does not concede it, 361,12-16. On the contrary, the nature of the universe fits it to share in God's benefits.

Simplicius found the 'natural destructibility' view in his earlier source, Alexander. Alexander argued, 359,11-360,3, that what is, like Plato's universe, destructible of its own nature, rather than contingently, is incapable of not being destroyed. Moreover, Alexander sides with those who deny that God can bring about the impossible. Plato himself had in the *Timaeus* put restrictions on God's power, 47E-48E; 75A. God cannot, for example, protect us with thicker skulls, while also allowing us sharp perception.

Simplicius protests that this argument would prove too much, 360,4-

29. For Alexander's leader, Aristotle himself, allows in *Physics* 8.10 that God overrides the natural tendency of the universe to stop moving. Indeed, on the interpretation that Simplicius inherits from Ammonius, Aristotle intends that God also overrides the natural tendency of the universe to disintegrate.

Textual Emendations

292,9: Reading *hikanôs*, with Ec and the MSS of Aristotle, in place of *kalôs*, as attested by the other MSS of Simplicius
295,24: Perhaps read *kai gar kaiper* for *kai gar kai* (in which case *phêi* should probably be read for *phêsin* in 295,25)
298,2: Perhaps read *legoi* in place of *legoien*
298,6: Perhaps read *pthartôi* in place of *apthartôi*
298,12: Perhaps seclude *homologountos*, or read *homologoumenou*
298,32: Reading *huparkhonta* for *huparkhon* of the MSS
301,7-9: Marking *alla kai to katêgorein ... to einai ekhein* as a quotation (of 298,16-18)
302,33-303,1: Read *ginomenon* in place of *genomenon*
304,19: Add *ê gê* after *pur*
304,33: Read *kai kata khronon* with c in place of *kai khronon*
305,6: Possibly read *kai kata khronon, diorizousan* for *kai khronon diorizonta*
306,3: Delete Heiberg's question-mark in favour of a full stop
307,21-2: Perhaps transpose *teleioteron* and *atelesteron*
310,10-12: Mark *ouden alloioteron ... tên morphên* as a quotation (*Cael.* 1.10, 280a12-14)
310,23: Mark *hoi tês diatheseôs hekateras aitiôntai to enantion* as a quotation (*Cael.* 1.10, 280a18-19)
311,2-3: Delete *kai hoti agenêtos kai apthartos estin ho kosmos*
314,13-14: Read *kathaper enioi ... legontes legôn; ou gar einai ginesthai phasin* for *kathaper enioi ... legontes legôn; ou gar einai ginesthai phêsi* as printed by Heiberg; *legôn* most MSS; *legontes* E²; *phasin* Aristotle, 280b9
314,21-2: Mark *holôs adunaton genesthai* as a quotation (280b11)
317,18: Reading *adunaton* with c, for *dunaton* of the MSS of Simplicius here
323,12: Reading *diplasia* for the MSS *diplasiôn*
323,19: Omit *to de haplôs*, with A
324,24-5: *oude to hupothesthai pseudos tauton esti tôi adunaton hupothesthai* should probably be secluded, as in bc
326,26: Perhaps read *phtharomenon* for *phtheiromenon* of the MSS
328,26: Read *einai dunasthai* with A in place of *dunasthai einai* (CE²b, Heiberg) or *dunasthai* (DE)

331,20: Insert *kai to aei einai* after *dioti*; perhaps read *hôste to mê aei mê on kai mê aei on* in place of *hôste kai to mê aei mê on kai to mê aei on*
333,13: Read *tis* for *ho ti*
336,6: Insert *to* before *aphtharton*
336,11: Read *to phtharton* with D, in place of *phtharton*
337,31: Read *tôi de* with c, against *to de* of the MSS
337,32: Read *to de* with c, against *tôi de* of the MSS
340,6: Read *alla hêi* with c for *alla ei* of the MSS
342,22: Perhaps add *khronon* after *apeiron*
345,35: Reading *tôi E*, with Eb, for *to E* of ADE², as printed by Heiberg
349,6: Possibly seclude *ê mê einai kai einai*
352,26: Reading *kath' ho* for *kath' hous* (Heiberg and most MSS; *kath' hou* D)
359,25-6: Extend quotation to finish after *ex anankês*
361,4: Perhaps read *tôn skhêmatôn* for *tou skhêmatos*
361,5-6: Read *kai theia kath' hauta* for *kai kath' hauta*
361,7: Reading *endidomenês* with A in place of *endidomena*
361,8-9: Read *hôsei* in place of *ei*; or seclude the clause *hôs upostas kath' hauton ên*

SIMPLICIUS
On Aristotle
On the Heavens 1.10-12

Translation

Simplicius' Commentary on Book One of Aristotle's 'On the Heavens'

[Chapter 10]

279b4-12 Having made these distinctions,[1] [let us say next whether it is ungenerated or generated, and indestructible or destructible, having first run through the opinions of others, since difficulties of contrary types arise in the demonstration of contrary things. At the same time, what we are about to say will also be more credible to people who have already heard the contentions of those who dispute them; for it will seem less the case that our case is won by default. Indeed, they need to be judges rather than legal adversaries] if they are to make an adequate[2] judgement of the truth.

Having set himself to show two things about the world, that it is unique and that it is ungenerated and indestructible;[3] and having shown the first,[4] he now turns to the remaining one, first of all (as is his habit) examining the opinions of others about the matter, which appear to be multiform.[5] For some say that it is generated but indestructible,[6] some that it is ungenerated and indestructible,[7] some that it is generated and destructible;[8] for no one has dared to affirm as a matter of opinion that it is ungenerated but destructible. Aristotle always seems to do this, namely examining the opinions of others first;[9] but in this case he also begins by setting out in addition the functions that this has for us, which are three or four in number.[10]

The first and most important is that it is not possible to come by the truth without first having confronted difficulties in many forms, as he also teaches in other works.[11] And the demonstrations of one type of opinion [create] difficulties for their contraries. For those arguments which seem to demonstrate that the world is generated become problems for those showing it to be ungenerated. Consequently, let him who seeks to overcome the difficulties examine those opinions that are contrary to one another, and the arguments which set them up.

The second benefit is the fact that what we say will seem more credible to our audience when they have heard not only our views, but also the speeches in advocacy (that is the demonstrations) of both of the arguments which are disputed and which are the subject of investigation in the case, both ours and those contrary to them. This provides for our audience both the more precise learning [that comes] by way of the solution of the difficulties, and a firmer conviction, since, as we are not ignorant of these things,[12] it would seem to be less the case that we secure votes against our opponents by default if we present their demonstrations and overcome them as far as possible, which is what Plato does most of all. For no Callicles, Thrasymachus, or Protagoras presented his own arguments as persuasively as Plato does on their behalf.[13]

He says 'the case is won'[14] instead of 'securing votes',[15] which means the same as 'winning the case',[16] employing the passive in place of the active. And he rightly adduces the reason why one should not secure votes by default: for, as he says, 'they need to be judges rather than legal adversaries if they are to make an adequate judgement of the truth'. And how can someone make a judgement who has not listened to opposing arguments?

279b12-17 Everybody says that it came to be, [but some hold that it is generated and eternal, while others think that is destructible just like anything else which has a natural constitution, while others still hold that it is alternately at some times in one condition and at others in another, and that it continues like this always, as Empedocles of Acragas] and Heraclitus of Ephesus hold.

Having spoken of what is common to the opinions of his predecessors, he then brings up their differences in this way. For he says that all of the natural scientists and theologians are of the same opinion regarding the generation of the world;[17] but of those who say that it came to be, some say that it is eternal, such as Orpheus and Hesiod,[18] and after them Plato too, as Alexander says. However, some of those who say that it is generated say that it is destructible [too], and this in two ways. For some of them say that it is destructible in the same way as anything else composed of atoms, such as Socrates, for example, who once having been destroyed is no longer capable of recurring.[19]

Others, however, hold that the same thing is alternately generated and destroyed, and having come to be again it is destroyed again, and that such a sequence is eternal, as Empedocles says that Love and Strife take turns to gain the upper hand, the former collecting everything into one and destroying the world of Strife and producing a sphere out of it, while Strife then separates the elements once again and produces the same sort of world [as before]. Empedocles indicates these things when he says:

> at one time all coming together into one by Love,
> at another each borne apart by the hatred of Strife ....[20]
> and again they become many as the one grows apart,
> so far they are generated and there is no eternal life for them;

but insofar as they do not abandon their continuous change, thus far are they always, and are unchanged in the cycle.[21]

Heraclitus too says that the world is at one time engulfed in fire, at another reconstituted again out of the fire, at regular intervals of time, in the passage where he says 'kindled in measures and extinguished in measures'.[22] Later on the Stoics too were of the same opinion[23] – but let us pass over them. It is obvious that the theologians speak of the generation of the world not [in the sense of its coming] from a temporal beginning,[24] but as [coming] from a productive cause, and they do so figuratively, as they do in other contexts.[25]

Empedocles indicates that there are two worlds, the one unified and intelligible,[26] the other separated and perceptible; and I believe that elsewhere[27] I have adequately shown on the basis of his own words that in this world he sees both the unification and the discrimination.[28] And Heraclitus, who also purveys his wisdom through riddles, does not mean what most people suppose; at any rate, having said those things which apparently concern the generation of the world, he wrote the following as well: 'this world ... no god or man made, but it has been always'.[29]

However Alexander, wishing to have Heraclitus say that the world is generated and destroyed, takes this to mean something other than the current world. 'For he [sc. Heraclitus] does not', he says, 'utter conflicting statements, as someone might think, since', he says,

> by 'world' here he does not mean *this particular* cosmic ordering, but existing things in general and their arrangement, in relation to which the totality changes into each of them serially, at one time into fire,[30] at another into this sort of world. For serial change of this kind and the world in this sense did not begin at some particular time, but has always existed.

Alexander adds the following:

> when people speak of the totality as being at one time thus and at another otherwise, they are talking of alteration of the totality rather than of its generation and destruction. Those who talk of the world as being generated and destroyed,

he says,

> as if it were like any of the other composite things, would be Democritus and his circle.[31] For just as, according to them, everything else is generated and destroyed, so too is each of the infinite number of worlds. And just as in the case of the other things what comes to be is not the same as what has been

destroyed, except in respect of form, they say the same thing applies in the case of the worlds.[32]

But if the atoms remain the same (since they are unaffectible), it is clear that they too should speak of alteration rather than destruction of the worlds, as Empedocles and Heraclitus apparently do.[33] A short citation from Aristotle's writings on Democritus will make these men's views clear:

> Democritus considers the nature of eternal things to be small substances infinite in number, for which he assumed a distinct place infinite in extent. And he assigned the names 'void', 'nothing', and 'the infinite' to the place, 'thing',[34] 'solid', and 'being' to each of the substances. He thinks the substances to be so small as to escape our senses, and that there belong to them every sort of shape and every sort of figure and difference in size. So he thought that visible and perceptible masses came to be and coalesced from these as from elements. These conflict with one another and move within the void on account of their dissimilarity and the other differences mentioned, and as they move, they collide and intertwine with such an intertwining as to make them touch and be next to one another, but which does not in reality generate any other single nature from them at all; for it is completely ridiculous for two or more ever to become one. And he attributes the cohesion of the substances up to a certain point to the way the bodies entangle with and embrace one another; for some of them are uneven, some hooked, some concave, some convex, while others have innumerable other differences. So he thinks that they hold together and cohere among themselves until such a time as some stronger compulsion comes upon them from their surroundings and shakes them and forces them apart from one another. He speaks of this generation and of the discrimination which is contrary to it not only in the case of animals, but also in that of plants and worlds, and in general in the case of all perceptible bodies.[35]

So if generation is a concatenation of atoms while destruction is the discrimination [of them], on Democritus' account too generation will be alteration. Moreover [although][36] Empedocles does not say that what comes to be is the same as what has been destroyed, except in respect of form, nevertheless even Alexander[37] says that he supposes that this is alteration and not generation. And I think that one should note in this regard that none of the ancients who talked of the destruction of the world were saying the same thing as those of our contemporaries who say that once destroyed it can never again recur.[38]

279b17-21 To say that it came to be and yet nevertheless is eternal [is to enunciate an impossibility. Only such things as we see to obtain for the most part or invariably can be reasonably assumed – but in this case the opposite is the case,] since everything that comes to be is clearly also destroyed.

Having recorded the opinions concerning the generation and destruction of the totality, and wishing to make a judgement among them, he turns to the first of those who posit that it was generated but is indestructible, among whom were the theologians[39] and Plato, as Alexander says.

It must be accepted that Aristotle frequently objects to the apparent [meaning of a phrase] in the case of archaic usage whenever in this more obvious meaning it does not agree with the truth. And he does this in order to help those with a more superficial understanding of the old arguments, since [he knows] that the theologians were speaking of the generation of the world figuratively, indicating the gods' ordering [of things] in respect of substance by [speaking] of what is earlier and later in generation.[40]

And Aristotle also knows that Plato speaks of its being generated insofar as it is perceptible and corporeal, because something of this sort, not being capable of dragging itself into being, has its existence as a result of something else which produces it, and moreover that it could not, on account of its being a corporeal substance, be at once a complete whole and yet still be coming to be rather than being.[41]

For this reason he writes in his epitome of Plato's *Timaeus*: 'he says that it is generated since it is perceptible, and he supposes that what is perceptible is generated, while what is intelligible is ungenerated'.[42] Thus it is not generated in the sense of coming to be at a particular time: for it is necessary for time to exist prior to things which are generated in this way, given that it came into existence at a particular time, as one might say six thousand or however many years prior to the present. But Plato clearly states that 'time came to be with the heaven'.[43]

So if there is a past time which entirely precedes whatever time is taken to be that of the present existence of the entity, in the same way as the future entirely follows it, time will have no beginning or limit, and neither consequently will the world, according to the man who says 'time came to be with the heaven'.[44] Consequently Aristotle's objections affect neither the theologians nor Plato, but rather those who interpreted the doctrines of the ancients in such a way as to suppose that, while the world was generated at a particular time, it was none the less indestructible. This is really absurd, and well refuted by Aristotle.

But Alexander of Aphrodisias does not understand Plato's doctrines as Aristotle understood them, nor does he accept that their views are in agreement, but having from the outset, so it seems, treated Plato's views as suspect,[45] just as shortly before our time some people [did with] Aristotle's,[46] he did not think the view itself worthy of correction, in the way that Aristotle, who does not mention Plato's name at all apart from a handful of times, none the less drags Plato himself up for correction. So it is necessary, and at all events only fair to Aristotle, as well as profitable for those who choose to understand and explain Aristotle's thought by way of his [sc. Alexander's] commentaries, to examine what he [sc. Alexander] said.

'For anyone would realise', he says,

> on the basis of what Plato actually says in the *Timaeus* that Plato was of this opinion, and that it is not the case, as some of the Platonists say, that the world, although ungenerated, was said by him to be 'generated' in [the sense of] its having its being in generation.[47] For something is 'generated', in the way that these people want him to have said that the world is 'generated', in its coming to be and being destroyed, but not in its ever actually having come to be.[48] But in distinguishing the things that are, he says 'what is that which always is and has no coming to be, and what is that which is always coming to be and never is?'[49] But in regard to the world, he does not say 'coming to be', but rather 'having come to be'. And at the beginning he proposes not to investigate whether it *is* coming to be, but rather whether it *has* come to be or whether it is ungenerated. Thus he says that 'we are about to construct our arguments concerning the totality, whether it has come to be or whether it is ungenerated';[50] and having proceeded a little further he raises the same question: 'whether it[51] was, having no beginning for its coming to be, or whether it came to be and arose from some beginning'.[52] And having set himself to investigate this, he proceeds to show that it did indeed come to be, namely that it arose from some beginning. For this was what was at issue; and there could be no [beginning for it] other than a temporal one.

> And in fact if what is coming to be has not yet come to be, clearly what has come to be is no longer coming to be. But he says that world has come to be; therefore it is not coming to be in itself.[53] Further, if he had said that the world is generated in the sense of its having its being in generation, he would have had to accept that it was destructible as well, since for something which is 'generated' in this way, destruction is assigned to it in the same sense as that in which it is 'generated'. But while he does hold that it is generated, he does not allow that it is destructible as well. For if they[54] were to say that it did not have its being in destruction, he could no longer maintain that it came to be: for this sort of generation is linked to this sort of destruc-

tion. And if he says that it is indestructible temporally, it is clear that he would be using 'generated' in the sense of 'temporally [generated]', since 'generated' in this sense corresponds to 'undestroyed' in this sense.[55]

Moreover, seeking to do away with the apparent consequence of its destructibility upon its being generated, he says that it is indestructible. So if he says that it is temporally indestructible, he would take this as being compatible with its being generated; however, this is not compatible with its being generable in the sense of its having its being in generation, but in the sense of its having come to be from a beginning in time. Therefore the world is generated in this sense according to him. And to seek a reason for its indestructibility, as Plato does, is, given that he agrees with this,[56] to say that it has come to be from a beginning in time. For if it were ungenerated, it would contain within itself the reason for and the origin of its indestructibility, at least if he agrees that what is ungenerated is also indestructible in its own nature.[57] But it is because the world is not indestructible in its own nature, that he attributes its indestructibility to the will of God.

Moreover, to predicate 'is' of the world is a sign of his not saying that it has come to be in the same way in which [he says] it has its being in generation.[58] For if prior to its having come to be it was not, while having come to be it is, 'has come to be' is not predicated of it in the sense of its having its being in generation.[59]

I have quoted all of this from Alexander so that those who encounter both it and what I am about to say [may arrive] at a judgement. So, since the bulk of what he said is directed towards [showing that] Plato said that the world was generated not in the sense of its having its being in becoming, but rather in the sense of its having come to be from a temporal beginning, it suffices, I think, to quote a single passage of Plato, parts of which Alexander himself also quoted.

For having asked 'whether it always was, having no beginning for its coming to be, or whether it came to be and arose from some beginning', he [sc. Plato] replied: 'it came to be: for it is visible and tangible and has a body, and everything of this sort is perceptible, and all perceptible things which are grasped by opinion along with sensation, are evidently both coming to be and have come to be'.[60]

You notice that he says that the same thing both has come to be and is coming to be, because it is perceptible? Moreover, the things which have their being in generation and that which has come to be coexist, just as the heavenly motion is both continuous and always in its end because, since its recurrence is always from the same place to the same place, any part of the circumference you take is both a beginning and an end.[61] And it is clear that, insofar as it is always in its end, it has come to be, while insofar as it is at a beginning and is in progress it is always coming to be; and consequently he uses [the term [sc. is generated]] of the world not only in the sense of its having come to be also in the sense of its coming to be.

In general, if he proposed to investigate only this about the world (namely if it has come to be and not whether it is also coming to be), as Alexander thought, why at the beginning did he distinguish 'coming to be' from 'being' but not from 'having come to be', when he said 'what is that which always is and has no coming to be, and what is that which is always coming to be and never is?'[62]

I wonder how it seemed right to Alexander not to take account of the distinctions between being and coming to be in regard to the world in order to discover whether the world is one of the things that [really] is or one of the things that come to be, when Plato had clearly presented them in this way. But since he had distinguished coming to be, but had said that the world had come to be, this man [i.e. Alexander] apparently thought it pointless to take account of the distinction between being and coming to be.[63] However, what he said *has* come to be he also says *is* coming to be.

And when Plato says that 'it has come to be and began from some beginning',[64] Alexander holds that this beginning is none other than a temporal one. But if there is invariably some time preceding what begins at some particular time (because the moment at which it began and which exists in a present time has a pre-existing past [time] just as it has a subsequent future time),[65] while Plato says that time came to be with the heaven,[66] it is clear that time neither precedes the heaven, nor did it have a beginning for its generation at some particular time.

We should then note what sort of beginning this is that Plato speaks of, namely that it is the productive cause. For after defining coming to be, he goes on to argue 'now everything that comes to be must come to be as a result of some cause'.[67] And again, having said that the world came to be and is coming to be and is generated, he concludes: 'now what has come to be must, we say, have come to be as a result of some cause'.[68] And the question is clear to anyone who looks for it: 'whether it always was, having no beginning for its coming to be, or whether it came to be from some beginning'.[69] For what is really real[70] is what it is and has no need of a productive cause, while what comes to be is so called in relation to some agent.

And if he [sc. Plato] was talking of this as a temporal beginning and cause, how can he say that this [sc. its existence] belongs to it on account of its being corporeal, taking this as an axiom?[71] Furthermore, although both Alexander and Aristotle before him say that the heaven is corporeal, they do not think that it had a temporal beginning. And this truly is an axiom: bodies that are moved by something other than themselves have their existence from outside and are for this reason coming to be, because they exist as a result of an agent.⁷²

But, he [sc. Alexander] says, if he had said that the world is generated in the sense of its having its being in generation, he would have to say that it was destructible as well, since for something which is 'generated' in this way, destruction is assigned to it in the same sense as that in which it is 'generated'.⁷³ Then did he not hear him [sc. Plato] defining 'generated' as 'coming to be and being destroyed, but never really real'?⁷⁴ For the motion of the heaven and its different configurations are always coming to be and being destroyed, and any substance which alters in respect of these things has both generation and destruction predicated of it.

But, he [sc. Alexander] says, if he [sc. Plato] is talking of temporal indestructibility, it is clear that he must also be using 'generated' in its temporal sense, since what is generated in this sense is opposed to what is destructible in this sense. But if Plato supposed the world to be both generated and indestructible, clearly he must have taken generability to be capable of coexisting with temporal indestructibility. Yet even before Aristotle, Plato says that what is temporally generated is also temporally destructible, in Book Eight of the *Republic*, where he says: 'while it is difficult for a state that is so constituted to be changed, still, since everything which comes to be is destroyed, not even this constitution will endure for the whole of time, but it too will be dissolved'.⁷⁵

And in general, if what is temporally generated is opposed to the temporally destructible, not simply as being generated, but as being generable and destructible in this way, and what is destructible is opposed to what is indestructible, then since Plato says that the world is temporally indestructible, he cannot have said that it [sc. the world] was temporally generated, since he knew that would be to say the same thing as saying that it was at once both destructible and indestructible.⁷⁶

Moreover, he [sc. Alexander] says, he [sc. Plato] takes its temporal indestructibility to follow from its being generated, and this, he says, does not follow from its having its being in generation, but rather from its having come to be from a temporal beginning.⁷⁷ I wonder how Alexander can say this: for indestructibility is consistent with generability in the sense of something's having its being in generation, but it cannot [be consistent with it] in the sense of its having a temporal beginning, given that what is generated in this way is certainly also destructible, and that it is impossible for the indestructible to be consistent with the destructible.⁷⁸

And I wonder no less at what he said next, namely that Plato makes God responsible for its indestructibility, all the while knowing that, since it was generated, it was by its nature destructible. 'For if', he [sc. Alexander] says, 'it were ungenerated, it would have in itself the cause and the origin of its indestructibility'.⁷⁹ For how could he not be aware that although Aristotle said that the heaven was ungenerated, he none the less held that it possessed a finite capacity in its own nature, and that he too assigned the responsibility for its eternal motion, which is equivalent to saying its eternality, to God?⁸⁰

'Moreover', he [sc. Alexander] says, 'to predicate "is" of the world is a sign of his not saying that it has come to be in the same way in which [he says] it has its being in generation'.⁸¹ But it is clear that if he does anywhere predicate 'is' of the world, he does so as a matter of normal usage (as we say of both the day and an age that they are), from the fact that, when speaking precisely, he wrote: 'what was and what will be have come to be forms of time, which we unthinkingly apply to the eternal substance, wrongly; for we say that it was, or is, or will be, but for it "it is" alone is fitting according to the true account, while "it was" and "it will be" are appropriately said of generation occurring in time'.⁸² And that he calls its substance eternal because it is intelligible and really real, is self-evident from what he says about the exemplar:⁸³ 'so just like it, it happened to be a living thing and eternal'.⁸⁴

I have said these things against Alexander for, while I respect the man and wish him well, I think that honouring the truth the more is dear to him too.⁸⁵ Aristotle, as I said, in setting out to refute the apparent sense of arguments⁸⁶ if it conflicts with the truth, first of all confronts those who say that the world is both temporally generated and indestructible by way of induction,⁸⁷ 'since everything', he says 'that comes to be is clearly also destroyed'.⁸⁸ Moreover, if it is necessary ever to posit something without reason or demonstration, those things alone should be posited which we see to obtain in many or in all cases, while in the case of what is now under investigation the opposite obtains, given that everything that comes to be from a temporal beginning is clearly also destroyed.

279b21-31 Furthermore, if there were no beginning [for the present state, but rather it was impossible for it to be otherwise through the entirety of past time, it will be impossible for it to change. For there will be some cause [of it] which, had it obtained earlier, would have made what could not be otherwise capable of being otherwise. And if the world was composed from things which were formerly otherwise disposed, then if they were always thus and incapable of being otherwise disposed it would never have come to be; while if it did come to be, then clearly these things were capable of being otherwise disposed and were not always thus, so that what has been composed will be dissolved, and it was composed out of things which were previously in a state of dissolution. And this has either taken place an infinite number of times, or is capable of so doing. But if this is true, it will not be indestructible, if it either at one time has been,] or is capable of being, otherwise disposed. 30

Having shown by induction that it is impossible for something which has come to be from a temporal beginning to be indestructible, he now shows the same thing by other means.

He confronts the hypothesis which holds that the world was generated from things which previously had a different disposition and which then changed into this world, and he adopts at the outset of the 35
demonstration the axiom which holds that, if something does not 302,1 have a beginning and the capacity for changing into something so that it is potentially the thing into which it changes, but rather is such that it cannot be otherwise disposed throughout the whole of eternity, then it is impossible for it to change. For if it were to change, there must certainly inhere in it some capacity in virtue of which it is also able to be otherwise disposed. For in everything which changes, the capacity, or thing potentially, is prior to the actuality.[89] 5

Having made this assumption, he applies it to the world. For if the world had come to be from some temporal beginning, and had been composed out of things (for instance, as it might be, from the elements) that were previously otherwise disposed, then, if they are always the same as they were previously, and [if they are] incapable of being otherwise, the world would not have been generated from them (since they did not change their prior state). But if the world has 10
been generated in the manner described by the hypothesis, then the opposite of the premiss is also true, namely that the things out of which it is [composed] must be capable of being otherwise and cannot always be the way they were at the beginning, so that what was previously dissolved will be composed [again].

And if these things are what were composed, namely things that were in actuality dissolved and had the capacity for not always being disposed in the same way, it is clear that even after the [process of] 15
composition they did not lose their nature, namely their ability to exist in a dissolved state and their capacity for not being always disposed in the same way. Consequently what has been composed *will* be dissolved, and the world will not be indestructible (given that it is assumed to be generable), but will be dissolved into those parts from which it was composed.[90] And not once only or twice – for why [should it be], given that the things from which it is [made] are 20
assumed to be ungenerated, or at all events indestructible? No, it was either thus or capable of being otherwise an infinite number of times.

And if this is case, it will not be indestructible. For what has changed and come to be from things which were once otherwise disposed cannot be indestructible since there remains, in those things from which it came to be and [still] is [constituted], the capacity for being the way they were before it came to be. For it does not also abandon the capacity for being the way it was before when it abandons being that way in actuality.

Consequently the whole burden of the argument is as follows. If the world is generated in time, the things from which it is composed have a changeable nature, otherwise they could not have changed into it. But if this is the case, it could not be indestructible, since it will return to them once more. But if the world is indestructible, it cannot have been composed from things which were formerly otherwise disposed; for if this were the case, it would not be generable. Consequently it is impossible for it to be at once generated in time and indestructible.

Alexander says that it is possible that he [sc. Aristotle] meant when saying 'if it either at one time has been, or is capable of being, otherwise disposed'[91] something equivalent in the first case to 'if the thing being generated[92] was earlier destroyed', and in the second case to 'if it was not previously already destroyed, but has the capacity for being destroyed, in that the things from which it was generated are of this nature'.

'But it is possible', says Alexander,

to argue with respect to the matter in hand in this way too: if what is eternal is incapable of being otherwise disposed, then what is capable of being otherwise disposed is not eternal. But the contents of the world can be otherwise disposed, given that they were generated out of the preceding capacity of things which were capable of being otherwise disposed. Moreover, the things from which the world was generated, if at any rate it *was* generated, were either eternal or not eternal. But if they were eternal and were always disposed in the same manner, they could not change, and consequently the world would not have been generated out of these things if it did not formerly consist of them. But if they are not eternal, they too were generated by something's changing. And if this is the case, they can change back into the things from which they were generated: for changes are from opposites and to opposites. So if the things from which the world [is made] are destructible, it too will be destructible.

These considerations, as I said, were deployed against those who say that the world was generated from certain things which pre-existed it, and [that it] had some temporal beginning, as Plato appeared [to say] when he said that [it came to be] from elements previously disposed irregularly. But he did not mean that the irregularity pre-existed it in time, given that he says that time was created along with the heaven.[93] And nor did he think that it had come to be at some time in virtue of itself; but, just as in the *Statesman*,[94] with the world already existing, he separated the Demiurge from it conceptually and saw it degenerating into disorder, so too anyone who wants to understand by hypothesis[95] what corporeal nature was prior to the shining forth of the demiurgic order would see it as being disorderly and irregular.[96]

And if someone wants to suppose the world to be generated in time, as some wise fellows of our time do,[97] saying that what it was composed out of did not pre-exist it, he is unable to offer a reason why it came about at that time, and not earlier or later.[98] For the things which are generated by change and which themselves change again into other things have as a cause for their being generated at that time the chain both of what precedes and what follows, while things [which come to be] from the non-existent cannot supply any reason for [their coming to be].

279b32-280a11 The consideration with which some of them attempt to support [their claim that it can be indestructible and yet have been generated is invalid. For they say that what they say about generation is similar to those who draw diagrams, not as of something generated at some time, but rather for the sake of exposition so that people may come to a better understanding, just like people watching the generation of a diagram. But this is not, so we say, the same thing. For in the construction of diagrams the results are the same if everything is posited to exist at the same time, while in the case of demonstrations of these things they are not. In fact it is impossible, since what is assumed earlier and what later are in flat contradiction. For they say that orderliness arose from disorder, and the same thing cannot be both ordered and disordered at the same time, but there must be a [process of] generation that separates them and [also] time]. But in the case of the diagrams nothing is separated in time. [That it is impossible, then, for the same thing to be at once eternal and generated is evident.][99]

It seems that the argument is directed in particular against Xenocrates and the Platonists,[100] because they say that the world was generated from the disorderly and irregular, since Plato said that 'God, finding everything visible not at rest, but moving irregularly and in a disorderly fashion, brought it to order out of disorder'.[101] So when these people say that the world is generable but indestructible, they say that generation must not be understood as being temporal, but rather as being said hypothetically, for the sake of exposition of the ordering of its prior and of its more composite components.

For in view of the fact that some of the contents of the world are elements while others are constructed from the elements, it would not be easy to understand the difference between them, and how the composite objects are generated out of the simpler ones, for anyone who did not mentally break down the composite into the simple, and did not examine how, if the simple things existed in themselves, the composite ones could have been generated out of them from a beginning.[102]

In the same way, in the case of diagrams, mathematicians who inquire into their nature break the composite [forms] down into simples, and examine how they could have been generated from them, given that they were generated from a beginning:[103] for example that the triangle [comes to be] from three straight lines joined together in respect of their angles, and the cube from six squares joined together in respect of angles and lines, and not in respect of planes.[104]

But perhaps natural scientists, who apparently hold that the world is generated but indestructible, and who say that it was generated out of one, two, or four pre-existing elements, also ought to explain its generation in this manner, as has been said. For in fact those who say that water, or air, or fire, [or earth],[105] or the four of them [together] are the principle, having broken down those things which now appear as composites, they posit these things [sc. the elements] before anything else as being the simplest, and, examining how the composites are generated from them (if indeed the world was generated from some temporal beginning), they say that it would be generated in this manner.

But Aristotle says that they do not properly explicate the generable, since the mathematical example is not appropriate for them. For the mathematician breaks things down into what is inherent in and always coexists with his diagrams: the triangle into three lines and the cube into six squares, things which always exist in them and require no change in order for a composite to be generated from them; but it is not necessary to assume these things as pre-existent.[106] Here, however, he says, things which are assumed for the generation of something cannot both exist at the same time as it does and preserve the account of generation: rather some things are earlier and some later, and they are oppositely disposed in relation to one another; and they no longer preserve a merely hypothetical generation, as in the case of the diagrams.

And these people say that ordered things are generated from disorderly ones, and it is impossible for the same thing to be at once both disorderly and ordered. Consequently it is necessary for generation to be real and in time,[107] so that some things pre-exist in time, while others are composed after them. But in the diagrams, the three sides do not pre-exist the triangle in time.

So just as no one would say that it was [merely] hypothetically that the intercourse preceded the conception and the conception the birth, or the stones and wood the house (rather they genuinely pre-exist it, and for this reason no one would call this sort of generation hypothetical, but rather genuine generation and time, which distinguishes[108] the things which pre-exist from those which emerge afterwards), in the same way, the generation of the world could not be hypothetical if the disorderly things pre-exist the world and cannot co-exist with it; rather the order must emerge after the disorder has been removed. But in the case of mathematics, even if it is impossible for there to be generation of the figures, 'generation' of a hypothetical sort is not impossible because of the invariable co-existence of the simples with the composites. I marvel at Aristotle's acuity here in not overlooking these sorts of [generally] disregarded differences among things.

However, since Plato defines what is meant by coming to be as that which has its being in generation and destruction but never really *is*,[109] and held that this belongs to the world because of its corporeal nature, he has no need of the aforementioned assistance with a view to saying that it is generated but indestructible. For while those who do need it posit its generation hypothetically as though [it came to be] from some particular time, he sees another form of generation in the world, one with which nothing prevents the indestructible from co-existing.

Plato, Empedocles and Anaxagoras and the other natural scientists clearly describe the generation of the composites from the simples in this hypothetical fashion, breaking down the things now observed into simples and explaining their composition from the simples, as if the things from which the generated things are generated pre-existed them in time.[110] In view of this, I think it should be said, against Aristotle's objection, that the difference between what can and what cannot be assumed merely hypothetically is excellently expounded, namely that in cases where the things from which generation is said [to take place] invariably co-exist with it,[111] it is always possible to assume hypothetically the prior existence of the simpler [bodies] and temporal generation; but in those cases in which it is not possible for the things from which generation [occurs] to co-exist with what is generated, but where they are oppositely disposed in relation to them, the things from which generation [occurs] must pre-exist them in time, and this is genuine, temporal generation, and not hypothetical generation. These things then may be accepted as being well said.

But perhaps even the principles of the natural scientists, for instance water, or air, or the four elements, continue always to exist in the things composed from them.[112] Empedocles, indeed, says that generation and destruction is nothing else

but simply mixture and interchange of what is mixed.[113]

And the other natural scientists also say that the world did not come to be through the destruction of water, or air, or the intermediate,[114] but rather with the simple things, from which the composites come to be and into which they are broken down, [continuing] to exist in it.

In the same way, Aristotle himself, in theorising the four elements in the world, and prior to them qualityless body and qualities, and prior even to them matter and form,[115] and saying that the more composite things always come to be from those which are primarily simpler,[116] would not, I think, have been prevented from assuming a hypothetical temporal generation. For the alteration of the elements and the eternal change of everything in the world would not have prevented him from saying, as indeed he did say, that in taking on qualities the qualityless body *produced* the four elements, and these in combination *produced* animals and plants.[117]

But Plato, he [sc. Aristotle] would have said, holds that the world was generated from disorder, and it is impossible for order and disorder to co-exist.[118] Consequently it [sc. disorder] was assumed to pre-exist hypothetically; however, it was not supposed to have pre-existed it temporally and then have been destroyed, but rather to exist always in the nature of matter, in its privation of form that dominates it;[119] it [sc. the disorder], then, is put in order by means of the demiurgic production of form. And just as according to Aristotle the formless inheres in the nature of matter, even though it always participates in some form,[120] so also material disorder co-subsists in it, even though it always has a share of order due to the demiurgic production of form.

And as evidence that Plato adhered to this conception in regard to that disorder which always co-exists in matter, I adduce what he also wrote in the *Statesman*, in which, having separated the Demiurge from the world conceptually, he considered it as once again moving in a disorderly fashion. He says in that passage: 'the helmsman let go of the tiller and withdrew to his own vantage-point, and fate and innate desire turned the world upside down again'.[121] Then he continues by saying

> as it turned back and clashed together the opposing impulses of the beginning and the end,[122] it produced a great earthquake within itself, and wrought another destruction for all of the animals;[123]

and proceeding further:

> the cause of these things in it was the corporeal element in the mixture, the companion of its nature of long ago, because it had a share of the great disorder before it entered into this current world. For it possesses everything fine as a result of its com-

poser; but from its former state it both possesses for itself whatever is hard and unjust in the heaven, and brings them about for animals.[124]

Consequently, since in Plato's view the disorder exists within it, just as privation does, nothing prevents him from talking of the generation of the world hypothetically. Aristotle, however, assuming the generation to be temporal, rightly concluded that it was impossible for it both to be and to be generated.[125]

280a11-23 To have it alternately coalesce and dissolve [is to do nothing other than to establish it as eternal but changing in its form, just as if one were to consider a man coming to be from a child and a child from a man as at one time being destroyed and at another existing. For it is clear that it is not any chance arrangement and constitution that comes to be when the elements coalesce with one another, but the same one, particularly according to those who uphold this doctrine, who assign to each of the states an opposite cause. Consequently, if the whole body, being continuous, is at one time disposed and arranged this way and at another that, and the constitution of the whole is the world and the universe, then it is not the world that will be generated or destroyed,] but rather its dispositions.

After arguing against those who say that the world is generated but indestructible, he turns to those who also hold that it is generated, but also [think] that when it has been destroyed it is regenerated again in turn, and this continuously, as Empedocles and Heraclitus, and after them some of the Stoics, seem to have said.[126]

Aristotle says that people of this sort too do not say that the world is destroyed, but rather preserve it forever, and simply ascribe alteration to it, having it change only in regard to its shape. For if the world is all the matter [there is] endowed with form and put in order, and if even when they say it has been destroyed it has form (only rather more completely, as it were, than incompletely),[127] in describing this as the destruction of the world they are saying something of the same kind as if someone were to think that a man who comes to be from a child and a child from a man was destroyed at one time and exists at another, since it is in this way that the world remains as a world through the changes. For the world does not exist in its having some particular determinate shape, since in that case even the changes and transformations of the elements into one another, and the successions of the seasons, would be destructions of the world.[128]

But if Plato were generated from Socrates' destruction, and then Socrates once more from Plato's, no one would call this the generation and destruction of a man as a man, but rather a change to an

308,1 alternate shape, particularly since the elements out of which they are both composed remain the same. In the same way, if there were to be generated from this world another world called a sphere,[129] or, as our contemporaries say, 'the new one',[130] and then this again [were to be generated] from that, this would be an alteration of the world, not
5 generation or destruction. And even if Love makes the sphere by gathering together the elements of this dissolved world, what forms the world is the commingling arrangement of the elements, and not any chance one, just as that brought about by Strife is a dispersing arrangement, and not any chance one, but is world-producing and always the same in form. The world could only be said to have been destroyed if the change occurred by way of their being turned into
10 things disordered and otherwise disposed in some way. But if each of them is a world, then both of them always have the same form; for there is something which makes all of the differences in the world always remain the same.[131] So how could this be the destruction of the world?

He says that it particularly follows for Empedocles that each of the worlds will always have the same form, as he [sc. Empedocles] says that the same determinate things are the causes, albeit opposites, of
15 the generation and destruction, namely Strife and Love. For if the causes are always the same and the matter is the same (namely the four elements, which are indestructible), then the arrangement that comes to be as a result of each of them must be determinate, always the same, and never in any way different.[132]

Consequently, if a world is the composition and ordering of the underlying continuous body (and not this particular [ordering], but
20 any one, without specification), it is clear that even when the whole continuous body is now arranged and ordered this way, and now that, it is not the world which comes to be and is destroyed, but rather its dispositions.

280a23-34 For it is impossible for the world as a whole, having been generated, to be destroyed [and not to recur again, if there is only one of them. For before its coming to be there must always have existed the composition before it, which not having come to be could not, as we have said, change; it is more possible [for this to occur] if they are infinite in number. But whether this is possible or impossible will become clear from later considerations: for there are some people for whom it seems to be possible that something ungenerated can be destroyed, and something which has been generated can continue to be indestructible, as in the *Timaeus*. For there he says that the universe has been generated, notwithstanding the fact that it will continue to exist for the remainder of time. In regard to the universe, so far we

Translation 21

have only argued against them in physical terms; when we have examined everything in general terms,] things will become clear about this too.

He turns to the third [possible] view of those who posit that the world 25 is generated, namely that which maintains that the one which has been generated is destroyed, but not in such a way as to recur again, but rather as we say of each destructible thing that it is destroyed, like Socrates for example. For it is not the case that Socrates, once destroyed, comes to be Socrates once again.[133]

For things to be thus, he says, is impossible if one posits a single world, but it goes through if they are infinite [in number]. And he 30 vigorously argues that the reason for its being impossible for a single [world] to be thus disposed is something of the following sort: for the matter, he says, and in general the composition and the nature out of which the world was generated, existed even before the world was 309,1 generated and was capable of changing into it; and from its being thus disposed the world came to be, since it had the capacity of changing into a world.[134]

Consequently too when the world is destroyed it reverts to that composition from which it came to be, which has the capacity for generating a world out of itself,[135] since this is what it was formerly. 5 But if this is the case, then a world will be regenerated out of it just as before. For something that has the capacity for coming to be something will in an infinite time come to be [that thing].[136]

Alexander explains the phrase 'which not having come to be could not, as we have said, change', which is genuinely obscure, differently, [as referring to] the ungenerated composition which, prior to the generation of the world, existed in that from which the world came to be, and which could not change into the world without generation, in 10 order that the world might come to be. And if [it came to be] through generation, then clearly this composition had the capacity prior to the generation of the world of generating the world, since all generation results from a capacity. From which it follows that even when the world is destroyed and reverts once more to this type of composition, this is once again endowed with the capacity of generating a world out of itself.

'The "which not having come to be"', he [sc. Alexander] says, 15

might rather be of the following kind: if the composition [existing] prior to the generation of the world were ungenerated and eternal, it would be incapable of change, since this holds good for it. But the world could not have come to be in this way; and since it has come to be, the composition prior to its coming to be was not ungenerated and eternal. Therefore what underlies it [sc. the world] can change into it and out of it, so that it [sc. the 20 world] will be regenerated out of it [sc. what underlies]. For whichever of these has been shown to have come to be, be it the world or that from which the world [comes to be], has been shown to recur.

I think that this is right on target; for if the world was generated in time, and the composition prior to it existed for ever before its coming to be, as something ungenerated but eternally existent, then we would deny that it could change into a world on the grounds of its always having been in the same condition. For this has been shown, namely that if something has not changed in an eternal infinite previous time, then it will not change hereafter.[137]

Aristotle says these things taking as agreed the fact that everything comes to be in a portion of time. This is, according to him, what coming to be is; something comes to be out of something else's changing, because nothing comes to be from the non-existent.[138] For this reason I have frequently said that it would be impossible[139] to assign a reason why something came to be then rather than earlier or later.[140] Those wise fellows of our time[141] who say that the world came to be from a temporal beginning, yet who think that there was neither any composition which preceded it out of which the world could have come to be nor that it was generated by change in any way at all, but rather that it came into existence from the non-existent, are unable to say for what reason it was created then, rather than earlier or later.

Then Aristotle, having shown that it is impossible if there is only one of them for it to be destroyed and never again recur, concludes that 'it is more possible if they are infinite in number'.[142] Alexander adds the reason: 'for', he says,

> it is not into the world's matter that there is dissolution and destruction for it, [matter] which had the capacity for becoming a world, but into another world; and since there is an infinite number of them succeeding one another, it is not necessary that there be a recurrence once again of the same one.

And this is the way it seemed to the circle of Leucippus and Democritus.[143]

It is easy, I think, to investigate how this hypothesis differs from that of alternate composition and dissolution, which Aristotle said 'is to do nothing other than to establish "the world" as eternal but changing in its form',[144] as Empedocles appeared to say. But perhaps this is more appropriate for Democritus and his associates, given that Empedocles held that the forms of his worlds were different,[145] so that he used different terms for them, calling the one 'sphere'[146] and reserving the word 'world' for the other; while since Democritus' worlds change into other worlds constituted from the same atoms, they come to be the same in form, although not in number?[147]

However, given that determinate productive causes were not posited for them, but rather they constitute their results on the basis of random atomic motion, the forms of the worlds which are generated may turn out not to be the same, but different in different cases; and for this reason the change will not be alteration, as it was for those people,[148] but generation and destruction. And it was perhaps in view of this that Aristotle said that the same ordering and constitution is generated for those 'who assign to each of the dispositions an opposite cause'.[149]

But if, as Alexander says, dissolution for Democritus and his associates takes place not into matter but into other worlds, how can this be an acceptable position for those who say that the worlds are infinite [in number], but not for those who say that there is single one of them, or many?[150] Perhaps then Aristotle, in dealing with the hypothesis of those who say that it is generated, but destructible in such a way as not to recur, did not assume that the dissolution would be into a world (since he has described that as alteration), but into non-existence, and it is this which he held to be unacceptable for those who posited a single world, but more possible for those who said they were infinite, since even though they are destroyed they will not be exhausted on account of their infinity.[151]

And he said 'it is more possible' not because it *is* possible to hold this, but with a view to making a comparison with those who say that it is unique and that it is destroyed in such a way as not to recur. For here the world would have disappeared, which does not happen in the case of the infinite [worlds]. That he does not think this thesis possible he makes clear when he says 'but whether this is possible or impossible will become clear from later considerations'.[152] For not only has it already been shown that the number of worlds is not infinite, on the grounds that body is not infinite, and indeed that there is no more than one of them,[153] <and that the world is ungenerated and indestructible>;[154] but he will also prove in the second book[155] concerning this [world] that it is ungenerated and indestructible.

'We should however consider', Alexander says, 'whether perhaps, in the later books, when he disposes of the atoms from which and as a result of which there results an infinity of worlds according to those who posit them, at the same time he also demonstrates this doctrine of theirs[156] to be impossible'. But perhaps, in order not to embark on a long digression, Aristotle says that it 'will become clear from later considerations', not because he is about to show that the number of worlds is not infinite, since this was already proved, but because he will speak of this in due order.

I adduce as evidence for this his employment of the reason-giving connective 'for'. 'For there are', he says, 'some people for whom it seems to be possible that something ungenerated can be destroyed, and something which has been generated can continue to be indestructible',[157] and in disposing of this he will show that the ungenerated is completely indestructible and the indestructible ungenerable, and conversely that the generated is destructible and the destructible generable.

And having shown these things, it will be established that, just as the generable cannot exist forever, equally the destructible cannot forever not exist, but must recur once again into existence. And if this is the case, then it is clear that it is impossible even for the things destroyed from an infinity of worlds not to recur any more.[158] And this is Alexander's suspicion when he says that there was concealed in the present argument a rebuttal of those who say that the world, once destroyed, will never again be.

As an example of those who hold that 'something generated might continue to be indestructible', he [sc. Aristotle] brought up what is said in Plato's *Timaeus*. For he himself makes it clear that he does not think that both propositions, namely that something ungenerated might be destroyed and that something generated might continue to be indestructible, are propounded in the *Timaeus*, when he argues: 'for there he says that the universe has been generated, notwithstanding the fact that it will continue to exist for the remainder of time'.[159]

'It is possible', Alexander says,

> to interpret what is written in the *Timaeus* as referring to both in common,[160] since it is of the same turn of mind to say that something generated is indestructible and something ungenerated is destructible. Moreover the disorder,

he says,

> out of which the world came to be according to them, being itself ungenerated, was destroyed when it changed into order and the world.[161]

But it is clear that, given that the disordered is, according to Plato, corporeal and visible (as he makes clear when he says 'God, finding everything visible not at rest, but moving irregularly and in a disorderly fashion'),[162] Plato clearly[163] says that it too is generated; for he has defined the visible as everything generated and generable.

So, perhaps, while no one has ever even given the impression of proposing this hypothesis, which has nothing to do with anything observable, namely that something is ungenerated but destructible, Aristotle still considers this possibility as well, both for the sake of completeness in division, and at the same time because the conversion of the ungenerable and the indestructible will contribute to showing that the generable and the destructible convert with one another too.[164]

Since Alexander claims here too that according to Plato the disorder of the *Timaeus* precedes the world, I too will recall once again that Plato says that time came to be along with the heaven:[165] how then could something precede the heaven in time? And he shows that the corporeal is, insofar as [it is considered] in itself, both dissolved and disordered, and (on the basis of God's goodness) eternal and organised, which is something Aristotle agrees with him about when he says that the world has in itself a finite capacity, but has become ever-moving and infinite in capacity because of the moving cause.[166]

'And against those who say', he [sc. Alexander] says,

> that the world is generated but indestructible, or ungenerated and destructible, he has earlier spoken in physical terms when he showed that the heaven was ungenerated and indestructible from the fact that every thing which is generated or destroyed is generated from its contrary and destroyed into its contrary, while there is no contrary for the heaven. For if there were some contrary to it, it would have the contrary of circular motion, since things which are physical contraries have contrary natural motions. So, having shown that there is no contrary motion to circular motion, he draws the conclusion that there is no contrary to the revolving body, and from this that it can neither be generated nor destroyed.[167]

This is a most physical demonstration,[168] since it is derived from the cause of the generation and destruction of physical bodies, namely that their generation and destruction are from contraries and into contraries.[169] But he has spoken only of the heaven.[170] But to those who have inquired generally about everything, whether it is possible that something can be generated and indestructible or ungenerated and destructible, the case will be clear in regard to the heaven as well; for the particular cases are demonstrated along with the general.

[Chapter 11]

280b1-6 But first of all we must distinguish [the ways in which we say 'ungenerated' and 'generated', 'destructible' and 'indestructible'. For the words are said in many ways,[171] and even if it makes no difference to the argument, thought will be confused if someone treats something which is divided in many ways as though it were indivisible.] For it will be unclear in respect of which nature what is said applies to it.

Having set himself to investigate whether indestructibility is compatible with generability and destructibility with ungenerability, since each of these [terms] is said in many ways he says that one must first distinguish their meanings, and properly, and he rightly expounds the usefulness of so doing. For in the case of things which are said in many ways, if one does not distinguish and define the meanings to [determine] which of them is the subject of the investigation, the thought of the listener must become confused.

And he adds 'even if it makes no difference to the argument' by way of reinforcement, because even then it is necessary to distinguish things which are said in many ways. When does the distinction of that which is said in many ways make no difference to the argument? Is it whenever it is known in what sense of [the term] the arguments will be developed? But even then, he says, the thought of the listener will become in a way confused, since he will vaguely have in mind the many senses [of the term].

Rather he says that distinguishing [things which are] said in many ways makes no difference to the argument of the speaker, whenever he constructs the argument about one and the same thing, and does not shift from one meaning to another, either for the sake of exercise, or sophistically.[172] For then, while distinguishing [things which are] said in many ways contributes nothing to the speaker's advantage, still the listener is unable to distinguish both when it is unclear and when it has already been 'proved', in respect of which sense the 'proof' has been made.

280b6-9 'Ungenerated' is said [in one way of something which now exists but previously did not, but without generation or change, as some people say is the case for contact and motion;] for they say that there is no coming to be touching or moving.

Having set himself to distinguish the meanings of 'ungenerated', he says that the first sense is that in which, although something previously was not and later is, it is none the less said to be ungenerated since it came to being without [a process of] generation, that is without any motion and temporal extension.[173]

For the things which need no generation for their existence are plausibly said to be ungenerated, as some say motion and contact are, thinking that contact comes to be immediately and without temporal extension, while in the case of motion they say that there is no generation and no change, and that it is not through generation or motion that the motionless passes into the moving. For if the motion is a change, there will be a change of a change and motion of a motion, and so on *ad infinitum*; and what he now attributes to others when he says 'as some people say', he himself has demonstrated in Book Five of the *Physics*.[174]

But perhaps contact and lightning, and in general things which seem to come into existence immediately and with no lapse of time, also have a beginning, middle, and end of their passage from non-existence to existence, and they pass into being by way of generation, and time measures their generation, even if it is so small as for its temporal extension to be imperceptible.[175]

However, motion and generation and changes, since they belong to other things which are moved, generated, and changed, do not in themselves undergo [anything]. For there are no journeys in journeys, nor extensions in extensions, nor are measures measured *qua* measures. But whenever we consider motion, generation, and change as forms that passed from non-existence to existence, then we conceive of their generation,[176] just as whenever we conceive of a measure, a cubit say, as being an extended body, then we say that it too is measured.

And yet, it is possible to say even in this case that, if there is a measure of a measure, one must proceed to infinity.[177] But [measure][178] is not measured *qua* measure, but *qua* corporeal extension, nor [is generation] generated *qua* generation, nor [is motion] moved *qua* motion, nor [is change] changed *qua* change, but only insofar as they too previously did not exist but later did, and hence changed in time. And it seems to me that Aristotle, because he conceives of such a kind of change for them,[179] attributes this account to others, saying 'as some people ... say:[180] for they say[181] that there was no coming to be [touching or moving]'.[182]

280b9-14 Another sense is that of something which can come to be [or have come to be, although it does not exist. For this is also ungenerated, because it is capable of coming to be. Another sense is that in which something is completely incapable of coming to be, and of existing at one time and not at another. ('Impossible' is used in two senses: either for its not being true that it can come to be,] or for its not doing so easily, or swiftly, or well.)

He offers as the second sense of 'ungenerated' that which can be generated, or progress into existence without generation (for which he said 'have come to be'),[183] but which has not yet come to be. Thus a house which can come to be is said to be as yet ungenerated, even while it is [in the process of] coming to be but does not yet exist.

He lists as the third sense of 'ungenerated' that which is 'completely incapable of coming to be'.[184] Since something can come into being even without generation (i.e. the first sense),[185] and this cannot have been coming to be, even though at one time it is and at another it is not, in separating the third sense from this he says that it is

25 'incapable of coming to be, and of existing at one time and not at another'.

On the other hand, he separates it from the second sense[186] by [writing] 'incapable of coming to be'; for he says that that 'can come to be or have come to be, although it does not exist'. This, then, is the genuinely ungenerable, and not in such a way as to be capable of
315,1 coming to be, and at one time being, at another not. Of things which exist, things ungenerable in this way are the eternal things, while of things which do not exist, they are those which are never capable of existing.

It seems to me that by adding 'completely', he indicates that the first senses pick out what is ungenerable in a way, but not fully. In
5 saying 'completely incapable of having come to be' he distinguishes two sorts of impossibility: the first, conceived in line with the 'completely', [is that] according to which it is not true to say [of something] that it could come to be in any of the senses of 'generable'; for the 'completely' does away with all of them. The other [is that] according to which 'incapable' is used broadly and loosely, in cases of things which come to be 'neither easily, swiftly, or well'; for this is said to be
10 incapable of coming to be and ungenerable in a broad and not very genuine sense.[187] So including this one there will be four senses of 'ungenerated'.

280b14-20 In the same way, 'generated' [has the sense of something which did not exist previously but later does, either having come to be, or without coming to be, not existing at one time, but afterwards existing. Or it has the sense that it has the capacity, either the capacity defined in terms of its truly [coming to be], or in terms of [its doing so] easily. Or it has the sense of something which exists and for which there is generation from non-existence to existence, either of something which already exists and which exists as a result of coming to be,] or of something which does not yet exist, but is capable of so doing.

15 Having given the senses of 'ungenerated', he turns to those of 'generated', saying that they are defined in the same manner as the former, because each [sense of the latter] is defined in relation to each [sense of the former], as they are properly opposed to one another.

The first sense of 'generated' he picks out [is that in which something which] did not exist previously later does so, whether through generation, or whether simply existing at one time and not at another, without [there being a process of] coming to be [for it], as is the case with contacts.[188] For all things of this sort are generable because
20 they exist later having formerly not existed, however different their mode of coming into being [may be]. This sense of 'generated' is opposed[189] to the second sense mentioned of 'ungenerated', in which

something which does not yet exist may come to be; for that which already exists although it previously did not, and is for this reason said to be generated, is opposed to that which does not yet exist,[190] and is for this reason [sc. so far] ungenerated.

The second sense of 'generated' [is that] which is capable of coming to be, whether 'capable' has been defined in terms of its truly [coming to be], or in terms of [its doing so] easily, swiftly, or well.[191] And this he opposes to the 'ungenerable' in the sense of incapability. To the first sense of 'incapable' [he opposes] what is said to be capable on the grounds that 'it may come to be' is true for it; that to the second [he opposes] what comes to be easily, or swiftly, or well; for this too is said to be capable of coming to be, just as that which does not come to be easily [is said to be] incapable [of coming to be].

The third and fourth manners of being generable he picks out are those in which the change from non-existence into existence occurs by way of generation, either when the thing is already in existence or when it is not yet in existence. And this manner is opposed to the first sense of 'ungenerated' mentioned. For that [type of being] ungenerated was that in which the change into existence was not by way of generation, while this [type of being] generated is that in which the change from non-existence into existence is not otherwise than by way of generation.

Thus Alexander[192] painstakingly[193] expounded and opposed the senses of 'generated' to those of 'ungenerated'. But perhaps the first sense of 'generated', which is the most genuine, is also opposed to the third [sense] of 'ungenerated'; and the phrase 'completely incapable of having come to be, and of existing at one time and not at another'[194] also makes it clear that this is the most genuine sense of 'ungenerated', given that something is generated which, while not existing formerly, later does, and which at one time exists but not at another, whatever might be its manner of passing into being.[195]

280b20-5 And the same goes for 'destructible' and 'indestructible'. [For we say that what existed previously, but later either does not exist, or admits of [not existing],[196] whether there is a time at which it is being destroyed and changing or not, is destructible. Sometimes too we call what is capable of not existing as a result of destruction 'destructible'. And yet otherwise what is easily destroyed,] 'destruction-prone' as one might say.

Next he provides a division of the meanings of 'destructible' and 'indestructible', beginning with 'destructible'. He says that the first sense of 'destructible' is that where that which previously exists, but which either later does not exist, or admits of not existing, whether it changes into non-existence by way of being destroyed, or without that, as contacts do. For the destructible in this sense is not said to be destructible on account of its manner of change, but on account of its existing at one time and not at another.

We must place a comma after 'or admits of', so that we may mentally supply what is missing, namely 'later not existing' (which the comma allows us to do).[197] And this sense is opposed to the first [sense] of 'generated';[198] for 'generated' is opposed to 'destructible' as its contrary, but to 'ungenerated' as its contradictory. And [something is] generated in that sense because previously it did not exist but later does, whether having come to be or without generation, and does not exist at one time but does at another, which he indicates here by 'whether there is a time at which it is being destroyed and changing or not'.

For this reason Alexander does not seem to me to be correct in holding that one might interpret the remark 'whether there is a time at which it is being destroyed and changing or not' as though he were saying that what is destructible is that which possesses a suitability for being destroyed even if it is not destroyed because something prevents it, like the chaff in uncut grain.[199] Rather here he means the opposite of what he meant in the case of the generated [when he said] 'either having come to be, or without coming to be, not existing at one time, but afterwards existing',[200] [when he says] 'whether there is a time at which it is being destroyed and changing or not'.

He offers as the second sense of 'destructible' a sub-class of the previous one, namely that which changes from existence to non-existence by a process of being destroyed, [a sense] in which contacts are no longer called destructible, and which is opposed to the third sense of 'generated'.[201]

He says that the third sense of 'destructible' is 'easily destroyed', which we are accustomed more properly to call 'destruction-prone'. This is opposed to the second sense of 'generated', in one of its senses:[202] it is said to be capable of being destroyed, whether 'capable' is defined [as meaning] 'truly' or 'easily'.[203]

280b25-8 And the same account holds for 'indestructible'. [For it is either what exists at one time and at another does not, but without [a process of] being destroyed, such as contacts, because without [a process of] being destroyed] they exist previously but later do not.

The first sense of 'indestructible' he picks out is that where what 'at one time it exists and at another it does not, but without [a process of] being destroyed'; contacts are of this sort 'because without [a process of] being destroyed they exist previously but later do not'. This is partially equivalent in force to the first sense of 'destructible'.[204] For what changed from existence into non-existence was said to be destructible, although not by way of [a process of] being destroyed, while this is indestructible even though it changes from existence to non-existence, since it does not do so by way of [a process of] destruction. And it is clear that the latter is 'indestructible' because of the manner of its change, while the former was 'destructible' on account of its previously existing and later not existing.

280b28-281a1 Or it is what exists and is incapable[205] of not existing, [or what, although at some time it will not exist, now does; for both you and the contact now exist[206] – but none the less both are destructible because there will be a time when it is not true to say that you exist,] or that these things are touching. <But most strictly speaking, [the indestructible is] that which now exists and is incapable of being destroyed in such a way that, while it now exists, it later will not exist or will admit of not existing. [Or indeed what has not yet been destroyed, but admits of later not existing.][207] And 'indestructible' can also be applied to something which is not easily destroyed.>[208]

'All of this passage',[209] Alexander says,

seems to virtually everyone not to be properly placed in the division of the indestructible. For it seems to designate a sense of 'destructible' and not of 'indestructible', since 'for both you and the contact now exist' signifies a sense of 'destructible', and it seems that the same thing is signified in the passage about the destructible which says 'what existed previously, but later either does not exist, or admits of not existing,[210] whether there is a time at which it is being destroyed and changing or not'. For this reason, some say that the scribe transferred this passage, which should have been written there in the division of 'destructible' as a second reading, and made a double mistake, both in not keeping it outside [the main body of the text] as a doublet, and also in transferring it from there.
But others,

he continues,

say that it *does* apply to the indestructible, signifying the same as what is about to be said, namely 'or indeed what has not yet been destroyed, but admits of later not existing',[211] and say that it has been improperly intruded into the text here, since in addition to that it makes a doublet. But it is not,

he says,

5   completely inappropriate for the division of the indestructible. For he seems in this passage to call what exists 'undestroyed' throughout the time when it exists, whether it is capable at some time of not existing or whether it will at some time actually be being destroyed and for this reason will not exist,[212] since it exists now; and we pay no attention to any of these things, apart from the fact that it does exist, and for this reason we call it undestroyed.

10   Thus Alexander. And that he [sc. Aristotle] calls what exists, when it exists, 'undestroyed' for the very reason that it now exists even though it will be destroyed, is clear from what he says a little later on, namely 'it has not yet been destroyed, but admits of later not existing'.[213] However, I do not think that the whole passage means this, since the beginning of the passage in most of the manuscripts
15   that have come down to me does not read, as Alexander wrote, 'or what exists but is capable of not existing',[214] but rather 'or what exists and is incapable of not existing'.[215]

Given that it is so,[216] he is now presenting the two senses of 'indestructible' rather unclearly, the strict sense by way of 'or what exists and is incapable of not existing', and the loose sense, of that which simply exists now, by way of 'or what, although at some time
20   it will not exist, now does'.[217] And he adds as examples of this sense 'for both you and the contact now exist', concluding that even though those things are said to be 'undestroyed' in view of their now existing, nevertheless they are still really destructible 'because there will be a time when it is not true to say that you exist, or that these things are touching', some of which will exist no longer because of [a process of] destruction, others without [a process of] destruction.

25   And having said these things rather unclearly, he goes on to present them somewhat more clearly. The strict sense [of 'indestructible' he presents] by 'most strictly speaking, what now exists and is incapable of being destroyed in such a way that, while it now exists, it later will not exist or will admit of not existing', which is opposed to the first sense of 'destructible'[218] and to the first sense of 'generated';[219] while the looser usage [is given] by 'what has not yet been
319,1   destroyed, but admits of later not existing'; and this is equivalent in force to the second part of the second sense.[220]

Finally he adds the sense of 'indestructible' in which something is 'not easily destroyed', which one might call 'destruction-resistant', to
5   correspond with 'destruction-prone'.[221]

281a1-17 If these things are indeed the case, [we should examine what 'capable' and 'incapable' mean. In its strictest sense, something is called indestructible because it is incapable of destruction, and cannot at one time exist and at another not. And the ungenerable is also said to be incapable (i.e. what is not capable of coming to be in such a way that earlier it did not exist but later did exist): for example, the commensurate diagonal. But if indeed something can move, or lift a certain weight, we always speak of it in relation to its greatest [capacity], for instance to lift a hundred talents or to walk a hundred stades (since it is capable of lesser amounts given that it is capable also of the maximum and so a capacity should be defined in relation to the limit and the maximum. It is necessary that what is capable of the maximum quantity is capable of lesser quantities; for instance if you can lift a hundred talents you can lift two, and if you can walk a hundred stades you can walk two. The capacity is for the maximum. Further, if something is incapable of a certain amount (speaking of its upper limit), then it will be incapable of any greater amount; for instance whoever is incapable of walking a thousand stades is clearly incapable of walking] a thousand and one.

After having distinguished the meanings of 'ungenerated', 'generated', 'destructible', and 'indestructible', he proposes to expound the senses of 'incapable' and 'capable', both because he had made use of them in the distinction of the meanings,[222] and because these things are indeed useful to him in clarifying the matter in hand (namely that there is nothing which has come to be which is indestructible, and nothing ungenerated which is destructible), since, as he himself will say, the strict senses of 'ungenerable' and 'indestructible', with which this discussion [is concerned], are defined in terms of impossibility.

For 'what is not capable of coming to be in such a way that earlier it did not exist but later did exist' is ungenerable. For the existence of a diagonal commensurate with the side is for this reason ungenerable, because if it does not exist it is incapable of later existing. And we predicate 'indestructible' in the strict sense of something which now exists and is incapable of later not existing. And 'generable' and 'destructible' too are defined in terms of the possible. For something is generable if, while it did not exist formerly, it is capable of later existence, and it is destructible if, while it exists [now], it admits of not existing at some time. So we need a definition of 'capable' and 'incapable'.

So he says that each capacity both is said to be and actually is in respect of the maximum and in respect of the greatest of which it is capable; for it is not capable of anything more than this. For if it were capable of more, it would not be this by which the capacity was defined; and nor is the capacity referred to by way of what is included or lesser, since it is not capable of this only. So the capacity which is incapable of walking more than a hundred stades, or of lifting a weight of more than a hundred talents would be the capacity for these things.²²³ For while it must be capable of what is within these things, it is not defined by them,²²⁴ but, just as the lesser weight is within the greater, so too the lesser capacity is contained within the greater; and the greater is proper to the greater capacity, the lesser to the lesser.

And just as the capacity is defined in terms of the extreme and the maximum of which it is capable, so too incapacity [is defined in terms of] the first thing of which it is not capable. But what Aristotle says in respect of excess is not the same as what he says in the case of the maximum of the capacity. For the latter signifies the greatest of which it is capable, while 'excess' signifies the first and least of which it is not capable, which has its existence in virtue of its exceeding what it is capable of. For someone capable²²⁵ of walking four stades is already incapable of walking five (which exceeds four), and is even more incapable of more. But five are the first which define the incapacity.²²⁶

281a18-27 This should not give us any cause for concern: [for let capacity in its strict sense be defined as being in accordance with the limit of the maximum. Perhaps, however, someone may object that what has been said is not necessarily true – for someone who can see a stade will not see all the magnitudes contained in it, but rather the contrary is true: the man who can see a point or hear a tiny noise will be able to perceive greater things as well. But this makes no difference to the argument: let the excess be defined in respect either of the capacity or of the object. For what is meant is clear: to be able to see the smaller thing is the greater [capacity], while in the case] of speed it is that of the larger [distance].

Having said that the capacity is defined by the greatest of which it is capable, and that someone who is capable of more is also capable of less, he conceives of an objection derived from the senses. For the senses seem to be inversely proportional to capacities, as Plato observed in the *Laws*,²²⁷ since the greater perception is defined in terms of the smaller things it can perceive, that than which nothing smaller can be detected. For the smallest visible and the weakest audible object are grasped by the stronger senses (since the greatest [are grasped by] any of them).²²⁸ And this is true not only in the case of sight and hearing, but in the case of the other senses too. The stronger senses are better able to detect the weaker properties in each case. Consequently, just as the capacity is defined by the greatest thing of which it is capable, so too the sense [is defined] by the smallest thing which it perceives.

And, resolving this objection before he has even brought it to light, he says 'let capacity in its strict sense be defined as being in accordance with the limit of the maximum'. Let the possible,[229] he says, namely that which pertains in all cases to the pinnacle of the capacity, not be defined by the greater or the lesser. For in this latter way, perceptual capacities will not be in agreement with the other [capacities]. For if the possible is defined in terms of the greater, the sense which can detect the smaller object will no longer be the more capable, and if [it is defined] by the lesser, that which is capable of lifting a greater weight or of walking more stades will no longer be the more capable.

But, he says, we must define the maximum of the capacity in all cases in terms of the limit of that of which the thing which has the capacity is capable, whether the greater or the lesser is the limit. In the case of weights, the limit is the greatest of which the lifter is capable of lifting. If someone lifting ten talents is capable of lifting twenty, thirty, and up to fifty, the limit of which he is capable is fifty.

But in the case of perceptible things, the smallest is the limit. In the case of someone seeing a finger-width, if he is capable of seeing a half of this as well, and a quarter, and up to a hundredth part, the latter is the limit in terms of which the maximum of the visual capacity is defined. Consequently the smallest is proper to the sense which excels, since the greater [power] is that which can detect the smaller. And the greatest is proper to the excellences of the other capacities, but the limit of what it is capable of is common both to sensory and to other capacities.

Alexander says that even in the case of perceptible things he [sc. Aristotle] says that one can characterise excellence of the perceptual capacity in terms of the greatest, provided that the magnitude is taken to be in the distances from which the sense can detect. For the greater visual capacity is that which sees from a greater distance, and the greater hearing that which hears from further away, and similarly with smell.

But first of all it is not the distance which is perceptible and of which it is capable in these cases, and in any case it [sc. distance] is not a factor for all the senses. For the sense of touch can be greater or lesser, but it does not detect anything unless what is touched is right up against it. Even so, the extreme of the capacity is defined even in the case of things touched by the limit of that of which it is capable. For the sense which is capable of detecting the smallest magnitude or figure, or the slightest hardness or softness, exceeds in capacity that which is not so capable. So even when Aristotle talks of 'someone who can see a stade', he is distinguishing the magnitude of what is seen, namely a stadium's length, not the distance from which what is seen is seen.

Having propounded the difficulty to do with sensation, and having shown how in the case of perceptible things, the smaller [quantities] define the maxima of the capacity, Aristotle says that it makes no

36   *Translation*

25 difference to the account offered of capacity and incapacity. For both the exceeding capacity the exceeding incapacity are greater, but the excess is defined by way of the capacity, whenever one exceeds and one is deficient in the same form, or in regard to the business of that which has the capacity.

But whenever the capacity is considered in and of itself, the account of the excess is simple. And whenever [it is considered] along with the thing which has the capacity, sight (and perception in general) excel in respect of the smaller thing perceived, while speed
30 does so in the ability to cover a greater distance in the same time. But the extreme of the capacity, whatever it is that the thing which is capable has, is an extreme, and what was said earlier is true, namely that any capacity is defined by the maximum in relation to the limit of that of which it is capable.

[Chapter 12]

322,1 **281a28-b2** [Having made these distinctions, we should turn to the next item.][230] If there are some things which are capable both of existing and of not existing,[231] [it is necessary that there be some maximum time determined both for their existence and for their non-existence, by which I mean a time in which the thing is capable of being and one in which it is capable of not being, whatever category they are in (i.e. man, white, three cubits long, and anything else of that sort). For if it [sc. the time] is not some particular quantity, but is always greater than any time posited, and it is not possible that there is a time than which it is shorter, the same thing will be capable of existing for an infinite time and not existing for another infinite time]. But this is impossible.

Having set out the things pertinent to the matter in hand, by making use of them he will go on to show that nothing generated is indestruc-
5 tible and nothing ungenerated can be destroyed. And he will show this after first showing that whatever one takes, be it substance, quantity, quality, or any other category, must, if it has the capacity for both existing and not existing, have each of those capacities for a determinate and not an infinite time. For if the time of its existing (and again of its not existing) is not determinate, there will be no time beyond it in such a way that the time posited will be less than a
10 certain time. Rather it will always be greater than any time posited, and so clearly it is capable of existing for an infinite time and not existing for another infinite time, which is impossible.[232]

So if what is said to be generated but indestructible is capable both of not existing for an infinite time before and of existing for an infinite time after, while the ungenerated but destructible is capable of

existing for an infinite time before (since it ungenerated) and of not   15
existing for an infinite time after (since it is destroyed), and it is
impossible for it to possess to infinity at the same time the capacity
for existing and for not existing, as will be shown, it is therefore
impossible for something to be both generated and indestructible, or
ungenerated and destructible.[233]

281b2-20 Let this be our starting-point: [impossible does not
mean the same thing as false. Impossible and possible, false and
true can be used hypothetically (as, for example, when we say
that it is impossible for a triangle to have two right angles if
such-and-such, or for the diagonal to be commensurable if such-
and-such); but there are also things which are possible and
impossible, false and true, *simpliciter*. And it is certainly not the
same thing for something to be false *simpliciter* and for it to be
impossible *simpliciter*: for to say, when you are not standing,
that you are standing is false, but not impossible. Equally to say
that a lyre-player who is not singing is singing is false but not
impossible. But to say that you are standing and sitting at the
same time, and that the diagonal is commensurable [with the
side],[234] is not only false, but also impossible. Thus it is not the
same to suppose something false and [something] impossible;
and the impossible follows from the impossible. Someone has at
the same time the capacity for sitting and the capacity for
standing, since when he has one, he has the other as well; but
not in such a way as both to sit and stand at the same time, but
rather at different times. But if something has a capacity for
many things for an infinite time, then it is not possible for these
to be realised in separate times,] but rather they must be   20
[realised] at the same time.

He begins the proof of the impossibility of something's possessing for
an infinite time, and concurrently, the capacity for being and for not
being by showing that the false and the impossible are not the same,
and that when something false has been supposed, it is not thereby
the case that something impossible has already been supposed; and
[by showing] that impossibility follows from impossibility, while
falsehood follows from falsehood, as he showed in the first book of the   25
Prior Analytics.[235]

That the false and the impossible are not the same he shows first
of all by distinguishing between their unqualified and their hypothetical forms, so that, having distinguished the many ways in which
they are said, he may select those around which he will construct the
argument, since in the case of the matter in hand he requires the
unqualified and strict senses and their mutual implications. Then, by   323,1
means of examples that are rather inadequately explained, he com-

pares what is in itself necessary with that which is hypothetically incapable of coming to be. For since the equality of the three angles of a triangle with two right angles belongs of necessity to it, it would be hypothetically impossible if someone were to suppose that the external angle of a triangle were not equal to the two internal and opposite angles, but either larger or smaller than them.[236]

And given that the diagonal of a square is necessarily incommensurable with its sides, it will be shown to be impossible if someone were to suppose that in right-angled isosceles triangles the side opposite the right angle is either double or equal to each of the sides which enclose it: for then if the square is completed, the hypotenuse, which becomes a diagonal, will be commensurable with the sides, being either equal to or double[237] them; but it is impossible for it to be commensurable, and the hypothetical impossibility is drawn as a conclusion from it.

But Alexander says that this example, of the diagonal's being commensurable with the side, is of something which is in itself impossible, but hypothetically possible. And it is possible to take it in this way, and in particular because Aristotle himself commits himself to talking of both, namely both of hypothetical impossibility and of hypothetical possibility, when he says 'impossible and possible, false and true can be used hypothetically'.[238]

And while he nowhere offered particular examples of things hypothetically true and false, we can tell from what has been said regarding the hypothetically impossible and possible how hypothetical falsehood and truth may occur. For if it is now day, it will be hypothetically false that it is day if someone supposes that the sun is below the earth; and although it is in itself false that it is now night, it will be found to be hypothetically true if someone supposes that the sun is now below the earth.[239]

So he omitted to give examples of these things[240] either because on the basis of what had been said about the possible and the impossible the account in the case of these was also clear, or because since there was no difference between the hypothetically true and the [hypothetically] possible, and the [hypothetically] false and the [hypothetically] impossible, the examples of the latter type were sufficient, as Alexander says.

Further, that the diagonal is commensurable, which is taken as an example of the hypothetically possible, would also be an example of the hypothetically true. For while it is in itself false that it is commensurable, it will be true hypothetically, just as while it is in itself true and possible that the triangle has [angles] equal to two right-angles, it will be hypothetically false and impossible, if someone were to suppose that the external angle of a triangle were more or less than the two internal and opposing [angles].[241] But perhaps even in these cases the false and the impossible are not the same, but rather the impossible is always false as well, while the false is not always impossible. For while it is absolutely true that I am sitting it will be hypothetically false if someone supposes that I am swimming. But it will not be impossible for me to sit, given that I am capable of sitting.[242]

After [treating of] things which are hypothetically possible and impossible, false and true, he explains which things are so *simpliciter* and in the strict sense, concerning which he will construct the argument. And in regard to these he is particularly concerned to show the difference between the false and the impossible, from which the difference between the true and the possible may also be easily understood. For to say of someone who is not standing but is capable of standing that he is standing is 'false but not impossible'; and it is possible, although not true, provided it is established that he is capable of standing at some time.[243] But to say that at the same time that he is both standing and sitting is, in addition to being false, impossible *simpliciter*. Similarly 'that the diagonal is commensurable with the side is not only false, but also impossible'. And by saying 'not only false, but also impossible', he indicates that while the impossible, in addition to being impossible, is invariably also false, the false is not *ipso facto* invariably impossible: for if they were reciprocally entailing there would have been no need to say 'not only false, but also impossible'.

And having shown that the false is one thing, the impossible another, he infers consequently that 'it is not the same to suppose something false and [something] impossible'<; and neither is supposing something false the same as supposing something impossible>.[244] It should be noted that supposing something impossible or false is not the same as saying that something is hypothetically impossible or false. For while someone who says 'let the diagonal be commensurable with the side' supposes something impossible, the one who says 'if the hypotenuse of the two equal sides which enclose the right-angle is itself equal to them, then the diagonal will be commensurable with the side' concludes something impossible from an impossible hypothesis. And someone who says, during the day, that 'if the sun is below the earth, it is night', says something false on the basis of something hypothetically false, the entailment holding in both cases.

Next he argues that the impossible follows from the impossible, and not from what is false *simpliciter* (unless what is false happens also to be impossible). He now posits this without demonstration because he has already shown in the first book of the *Prior Analytics* that the consequences are appropriate, so that that the false follows from the false and the impossible from the impossible.[245]

Then next he assumes something else useful towards the demonstration of the matter in hand, namely that something has at the same time the capacity for contradictories (such as for standing and sitting), but not indeed in such a way as for it to possess the actualities of these capacities at the same time (since it is impossible to actualise contraries at the same time), but rather so as to actualise them at different times and serially (although not at different [times] in the sense of [actualising them] at different determinate [times]),[246] such as for example the capacity of being young at one [time] and of going grey at another; for if it is like this, it no longer simultaneously possesses the capacities for opposites, since someone who has grown old is no longer capable of being young.

But whenever at some particular time it is no more natural for it to actualise the actuality of this capacity than for its opposite, then it may be said to possess both capacities at the same time, e.g. of standing and of sitting; but not indeed that it can actualise both actualities at the same time.

But someone who says that something has the capacity for many opposing things for an infinite time does not speak of it as though it is going to have the actualities at different times: for then it would no longer have the capacity for them for an infinite time, if there is some time when it is incapable of possessing the actuality of one of them. But someone who says this is saying that it is possible for something to possess at the same time the actualities of many opposing things, which is impossible. So if someone were to say that something possessed the capacity for being and not being for an infinite time, he would be saying that it was capable of actualising both at the same time, which is impossible, since it is impossible either to do or to undergo a plurality of opposing things at the same time.[247]

281b20-5 Consequently, if something which exists for an infinite time is destructible, [it must be capable of not being. So if [it has this capacity] for an infinite time, then let what it is capable of [sc. its not existing] obtain too; and so it will both be and not be in actuality at the same time. (So a false conclusion will result because a false premiss was posited; although if it were not impossible, then the conclusion would not be impossible as well.)] Consequently everything that is always existent is indestructible *simpliciter*.

Making use of what has been previously accepted, he goes on to show that the eternal is indestructible, and then that it is ungenerable, and then finally that these things convert with the eternal. That is, having undertaken to show that both the indestructible and the ungenerable are eternal, if the indestructible and the ungenerable do not follow from one another, he says, neither will being eternal be entailed by either of them.[248]

In order to show that the indestructible and the ungenerable follow from one another he shows first that the generable and the destruc-

tible are reciprocally entailing. And thus it will be shown in general, as was promised, that it is impossible for something which is ungenerable to be destroyed, and for something which has been generated to continue to be indestructible, given that the ungenerable and the indestructible are eternal, and that both the ungenerable and the indestructible and the generable and the destructible are reciprocally   10
entailing.[249]

Each of the three methods of reasoning[250] which he has used show what has been claimed. For if the ungenerable and indestructible are eternal, it is impossible either for the ungenerable to be destructible, or for the generated to be indestructible, since neither the generable nor the destructible are capable of being eternal. And if both generable and destructible, and indestructible and ungenerable,   15
reciprocally entail one another, then it will be impossible for something ungenerated to be destroyed, or for something generated to continue to be indestructible.

So first he shows on the basis of what has been said already that the eternal is indestructible and could not be destructible. It has already been accepted that something which has the capacity for many things for an infinite time, namely both for being and for not being, must possess them in such a way as to be capable of admitting both of them in actuality at the same time: for if there is a time when   20
it is incapable of actualising both of them, it will be vain to say that it has for an infinite time a capacity for both of them.[251] For every capacity is a capacity for some actuality: consequently what has an infinite capacity for not being (for this is what the eternally destructible has been supposed to be), since each capacity is a capacity for some actuality, would at some time be in a state of non-existence, and   25
the hypothesis that that of which it was capable is present for it in actuality will not be an impossible one.[252]

So let it be stipulated that it has been destroyed,[253] even if it has not yet been destroyed: this hypothesis will be false (if it has not yet been destroyed), but not impossible, given that it has the capacity for being destroyed. But if, while it is eternal, it is destroyed at some time, it must at the same time both exist and not exist, which is not only false but impossible too. But our hypothesis, that what has the   30
capacity for undergoing this is now, as it might be, destroyed, is not impossible but merely false.[254]

Therefore the impossible consequence does not follow from the hypothesis [itself] (since the impossible does not follow from the [merely] false), but from what was from the beginning completely impossible, namely that it could possess for an infinite time the capacity for not being. For someone who supposes that something   327,1
eternal is destructible says this:[255] for he says that something which always exists has the capacity for at some time not being, so that if it is supposed not to be it will at the same time both be and not be – and

what could be more impossible than that? It will exist, because whatever has any capacity at all for an infinite [time] must exist for an infinite [time] (since what does not exist cannot be said to have a capacity),[256] while it will also not exist, because it was stipulated to have undergone that of which it was capable.[257]

To make this clear, Aristotle adds 'so if for an infinite time'. For what possesses a capacity for an infinite time must also exist for an infinite time, whether it has the capacity for being or for not being (as Aristotle had assumed before in saying that it had the capacity for many things for an infinite time),[258] or whether it only has the capacity for not being.

So it was unnecessary, in my view, for Alexander to think it necessary to supply 'it has the capacity for both of them' with 'if ... for an infinite time' and equally 'namely that it both is and is not' with 'let what it is capable of obtain too'.[259] For it is sufficient for its existing for ever to suppose that it exists for an infinite time, but no less [to suppose that] it possesses for an infinite [time] the capacity for not being.[260] For to be destructible for an infinite [time] indicates nothing else than that it exists for an infinite [time]: for what possesses any capacity whatever as it were infinitely[261] is so;[262] and particularly [what possesses the capacity] for being and not being.

Concluding this argument, Aristotle says 'everything that is always existent is indestructible *simpliciter*', i.e. that which does not possess the capacity for being destroyed is not of such a kind as to be called destructible: the addition of the '*simpliciter*' makes this clear: for if what existed always was not indestructible *simpliciter*, but also had a capacity for being destroyed, or for not being, an impossibility would have been shown to follow, namely that the same thing both is and is not at the same time in actuality, which follows not from a false supposition, but from the impossible supposition that what is eternal is destructible. Thus he plausibly says in conclusion 'everything that is always existent is indestructible *simpliciter*'.[263]

281b25-33 Equally, it is ungenerable too, [since if it were generated, it will have the capacity of not existing for some time; for while the destructible is that which existed formerly but either now does not exist or possibly will not exist at some later time, the generable is that for which it is possible that it did not exist earlier. But there is no time either infinite or finite at which it is possible for that which always exists not to exist, since indeed if it is capable of doing so for an infinite time, it certainly is for a finite one. Therefore it is not possible for one and the same thing] to have the capacity of always existing and of always not existing.

Having shown that what always exists is indestructible, he goes on to show that it is ungenerable as well, now employing both a new method of reasoning and the one already used. So, on the supposition that it is generated, he infers that 'it will have the capacity of not existing for some time'. For just as we say that the destructible is that which is capable of not existing after it exists, similarly the generable is what is capable of not existing prior to its existence, while what is supposed to exist always cannot not exist.[264]

In fact, it is capable of not existing neither for an infinite nor for any finite time, since he who supposes it not to exist for that finite time supposes something impossible. For if it exists for an infinite time, which he says 'it is capable of doing', clearly it will exist for that finite time, since every finite [interval of time] is comprehended in an infinite one.[265] Thus, employing the concept of existing for ever, he shows that what always exists is also ungenerable, given that it exists always, while what is generable must at some time not exist.

Then he infers that 'therefore it is not possible for one and the same thing to have the capacity of always existing and of always not existing', reminding us of the demonstration already made in the case of the destructible.[266] For if something which exists always is supposed to be generable, then while existing in actuality it will always possess the capacity of not existing, since it is, while always existing, generable. Therefore, whenever we suppose that that of which it is capable holds of it, it will turn out that the same thing both exists and does not exist in actuality, which is impossible.[267]

And, intensifying the impossibility, Aristotle says: 'therefore it is not possible for one and the same thing to have the capacity of always existing and of always not existing'; for always not existing is the contrary of always existing, as we will learn.[268] So, having first shown by way of the concept of what always exists that it is impossible for it at some time not to be, now from the fact that what always exists and yet is said to be generable always possesses the capacity for not existing,[269] if this (which is possible) is made into an actuality,[270] it turns out that it always exists and always does not exist. For it does not possess the capacity for not existing for some determinate time, since before and after that it would no longer be generable,[271] but it is established that, just as it possesses the capacity for existing for an infinite time, so too does it for not existing.[272]

281b33-282a4 Furthermore, neither can it possess the contradictory, [by which I mean not always existing. Therefore it is impossible for something both to exist always and to be destructible. Nor, similarly, is it generable: for if, given two terms, it is impossible for the second to obtain without the first, and it is impossible that the first obtain, then it is impossible that the

44 *Translation*

25 second obtain. Consequently, if what always exists cannot at any time not exist,] it is impossible too that it be generable.

Having said that it is not possible for one and the same thing to be capable of both always existing and always not existing,[273] and having noted that always existing is the contrary of always not existing, since while they can never both be true at the same time, they are yet both false[274] of those things which sometimes exist and sometimes do not
30 (e.g., in the case of the atoms, those things which come to be and are destroyed),[275] he plausibly inferred that not only is it impossible for the contrary of always existing (i.e. always not existing) to obtain at the same time as it, it is not possible either for the negation (which says that it does not always exist) to be true at the same time as the
329,1 affirmation that it always exists: for it is not possible for [both parts of] a contradiction to be true at the same time. And if something which always exists is destructible or generable, it is clear that it does not always exist, so that the contradiction will be true at the same time for those who say that what existed always is destructible or generable.[276]

And since he first supposed that what always exists is destructible,
5 and then that what always exists is generable, for this reason he deals with the destructible first in the argument based on the negation too. And that not always existing is the negation of always existing is clear also from the fact that in all cases they are parcelled out between the true and the false:[277] for they are capable neither of both being true nor of both being false at the same time. And it is also clear
10 from the fact that assertions which contain an 'is' which also indicates the time become negations when a negative particle is added to 'is' and consequently that where the 'is' does not also indicate the time while something else is indicative of it, it is to the latter that one must add the negative particle in order for it to become a negation.[278]

So if, in the case of 'is always existing', the 'is' does not indicate the time (since in these cases the present time is not determined)[279] while
15 'always' is indicative of the time in such cases (for it is 'always' because it is throughout the whole of time, and not in some determined portion among many), it is reasonable then that the negation is created by adding the negation to the 'always', and the negation of 'is always existing' is 'not always is existing', while 'is always not existing' is its contrary: for it is furthest removed from it,[280] and while they may both be assumed to be false at the same time, they can never [be assumed to be] true.[281]
20 Moreover, the eternal seems to be a mode of existence, like the necessary; and in modal cases negations are formed by adding the negation-operators to the modal premises, as was taught in *On Meaning*.[282] So having said that, because an assertion and its negation are never true at the same time,[283] it is impossible for what

always exists not to exist always, for this reason he inferred that it is
impossible for something to exist always and yet be destructible 25
(since what is destructible does not exist always).[284] 'Nor, similarly,
is' what always exists 'generable', since, just like the destructible, the
generable too does not exist always, and for this reason the generable,
just like what does not always exist, does obtain at the same time as
what always exists.

And he shows the same thing by the abstraction [of the general
theorem] of the two terms.[285] But in fact I think that this argument
too depends upon the negation,[286] because he adds the reason-giving 30
connective, saying '*for* if, given two terms', etc.[287] For just as, if it is
impossible for Socrates to be a man and yet not be an animal ('man' 330,1
is posterior, while 'animal' is prior, being more general and universal), then were it impossible for Socrates to be an animal, it would
also be impossible for him to be a man. For how could the more
particular exist if what is more general and inclusive of it does not?

Similarly, as the prior and more general [category] is that which 5
at some time is and at another is not (which is equivalent to that
which does not exist always, which is the negation of that which
always is), while the generable is posterior and more particular
(because 'not existing at some time' belongs not only to the generable
but also to the destructible),[288] if it is impossible for what always
exists at some time not to be (i.e. not always to exist), it will be
impossible too for it to be generable. So just as it had been shown by
way of the negation that it is impossible for what always exists to be
destructible, so it was also shown by way of the negation that it is
impossible too for it to be generable.[289] And [it was] for this reason 10
that he said 'nor, similarly, is it generable'.

However, Alexander and the other commentators took the demonstration of the fact that what exists always is not generable to be
other than by way of negation, even though Aristotle, after having
shown by way of negation that what always exists is not destructible,
argues 'equally' what always exists 'cannot be generable', adding yet 15
another mode of demonstration by way of negation. The reason for
this[290] is, I think, that Aristotle, in the exposition of the two terms,
did not name the negation of what always exists as what does not
always exist, but rather, what comes to the same thing, what at some
time does not exist.

282a4-22 And since the negation of that which always has the
capacity for existing [is that which does not always have the
capacity for existing, while that which is always capable of not
existing is its contrary (whose own negation is that which is not
always capable of not existing), it is necessary that the negations of both [contraries] apply to the same thing, that is that

there will be an intermediate between that which always is and that which always is not, namely that which is capable of being and of not being. For the negation of each will obtain at some time, if not always. Consequently the not always non-existent will exist at some time and at another will not, and so clearly will that which is not always capable of existing; rather at some time it will exist, and at another it will not. Therefore the same thing will be capable of being, and capable of not being, and this is the intermediate between both [extremes]. In general, the argument is as follows: let A and B be incapable of belonging to the same thing; but suppose that everything is either A or C, and either B or D. It is then necessary that C and D must belong to everything which is neither A nor B. Then let E be intermediate between A and B (as they are contraries, what is neither [of them] must be intermediate [between them]) – it is clearly necessary that both C and D belong to it: E must be either A or C, since everything is [either A or C]. Therefore, since it is impossible that it is A, it must be C. The same argument applies to D as well]. So neither that which always exists nor that which always does not exist is either generable or destructible.

Alexander says that he shows by this that the generable and the destructible belong to the same nature.[291] But while this is true, this is not however the principal point; rather he shows by way of this the same thing [as before], namely that what always exists is neither generable nor destructible. For the argument terminates in the following conclusion: 'so neither that which always exists nor that which always does not exist is either generable or destructible'. And this is what has already transpired in what has been said.[292]

This argument, then, will contribute to showing that being generable and being destructible follow from one another, from which it will be shown that being ungenerable and being indestructible also follow from one another. So now to begin with he shows that neither what always exists nor what always does not exist is either generable or destructible from the fact that the negations of what always exists and of what always does not exist are true of some nature intermediate to both, which belongs to what is both generable and destructible.

For since, he says, 'the negation of that which always has the capacity for existing' – i.e. of that which always exists: for evidently he uses it to mean this in all cases – 'is that which does not always have the capacity for existing', while the positive contrary is that which is always capable of not existing, of which the 'negation will be that which is not always capable of not existing, it is necessary that the negations of both' the affirmations 'apply to some one thing' which is different from either of the contraries.

Alexander appended this last clause,[293] since it is possible for the negation of each affirmation to apply to the contrary affirmation: for 'not-white' holds of what is black, but 'not-black' does not also [hold of it]. Consequently, for the negations of both of the contraries to hold of something, it is necessary that this thing be something different from either of them, and we append this additionally, as it is lacking from the exposition. For it is necessary for negations to apply to that to which the affirmations do not, given that either the affirmation or the negation of things which are contradictorily opposed must apply to everything.[294]

And it is necessary, he says, that that to which the negations of always existing and always not existing apply is something intermediate between both affirmations,[295] which is capable both of existing and not existing, of existing because it is not always non-existent, and of not existing because it is not always existent. For the negation of each of them gets rid of the 'always', both from existing and not existing; and if it does not always [either exist or not exist], but admits of existing at one time and not existing at another, because it gets rid [both of its always existing][296] and of its always not existing, it follows that both that which is not always not existing and that which is not always existing will be at some time and not at another.[297]

Of such a kind are both the generable and the destructible, for which the negation of their always not existing yields their existence at some time, while that of their always existing yields their non-existence at some time. And such a thing, namely that which exists at some time and not at another, is really intermediate between what always exists and what always does not, since it participates in both existence and non-existence at some time. For, the negations which got rid of the 'always', still leave room for 'at some time'.

But he does not say this, namely that everything of which the negations of contraries are true will be intermediate between the contraries, since that is not universally true. For in the case of unmediated contraries[298] there is nothing between them, though in this case too there is something for which the negations of both contraries hold good. For being sick and being healthy, even and odd, seem to be unmediated contraries, and there is no intermediate between being sick and being healthy in respect of which it is true to say that [something] is neither sick nor healthy (although both are true of wood);[299] and nor is 'neither odd nor even', when it holds true of continuous quantity, predicated of something intermediate between odd and even.

But it needs to be investigated whether there are any unmediated contraries;[300] for that health and disease are not unmediated is clear from the fact that doctors refer to a condition which is neither,[301] while that there are intermediates between even and odd is evidenced by the 'even-odd' and the 'odd-even'.[302] And in general, if contraries are those which are furthest apart from each other in the same genus,[303] and if 'furthest' implies a smaller distance, there will be no unmediated ones.

But nor is it even true in the case of mediated contraries that whatever the negations of the contraries hold of is intermediate between the contraries. For the negation of both white and black holds of a point, but a point is not intermediate between white and black.[304] For in the case of mediated contraries the negation of either contrary in fact holds true of what is intermediate, without its being the case too that everything of which they hold true is intermediate. Nor did Aristotle assert this as a universal truth, but rather posited as universal that the negations of contraries hold true of the same thing, whereas something of which the negations of both of the contraries hold true turns out to be properly intermediate when the negations of what always exists and what always does not exist hold true of it.[305]

He himself appends the reason for this when he says 'the negation of each will obtain at some time if not always'; for having got rid of the 'always', both 'at some time's remain, namely that at some time it exists and at some time it does not exist. So in cases of things where the negations of the contraries hold true in such a way that those things share in the contraries in some way, those things will be intermediate between the contraries; but it is not true *simpliciter* that everything of which the negations are true [is like this].

Alexander investigates in what way what always exists and what always does not exist are contraries: for what could be the genus common to both? And he says that even if it were not accepted that all contraries of one another fall under the same genus, still contraries *simpliciter* and strictly speaking would be of such a kind. These things are said without concatenation,[306] such as white and black; but in cases of concatenation this is no longer the case, since contrariety is different in the case of propositions.[307] So just as 'of necessity it exists' and 'of necessity it does not exist' are agreed to be contrary propositions even though they have no common genus, so too 'it always exists' and 'it always does not exist' are contrary to one another in exactly the same way as the former pair: for 'it always exists' is equivalent to 'of necessity it exists', as 'it always does not exist' is to 'of necessity it does not exist'.[308] But, he [sc. Alexander] says, it is possible to speak of a common genus even for these, namely the proposition or still better the affirmation.[309]

So, he [sc. Aristotle] says, that for which the negations of both hold true, will at some time exist and at some time not exist. Therefore the same nature is receptive both of the capacity for being and for not being. And of such a kind are the destructible and the generable: for the destructible is that which is capable of not being, while the generable is that which is capable of being. Therefore the same thing will be both generable and destructible, given that the same thing is capable of being and not [being], as Aristotle says, and if the generable has it[310] in respect of the capacity for being, the destructible in respect of the capacity for not being, since that which is capable both of being and not being is one and the same thing, intermediate between the contraries. Consequently, then, 'generable', and 'destructible' convert.

He shows that it has been properly assumed that if the negation of one of the contraries is true of something the other will be [true of it] too in virtue of this, and that the argument is quite general, by way of letters,[311] as was his habit in the case of general demonstrations, having first determined what a general argument is.[312] He posits A and B as contraries, since contraries are things which are incapable of holding of the same thing. Then he assumes in addition the negation of each of them, C for A and D for B, and creates two contradictory oppositions, as he indicates by saying 'everything is either A or C, and either B or D' (for this is the defining characteristic of a contradictory opposition).[313]

Then if the assertions A and B are contraries,[314] and C and D, their negations, are contradictorily opposed to them, 'it is then necessary that C and D must belong to everything which is neither A nor B', given that of propositions which are contradictorily opposed to one another it is necessary that either the affirmation or the denial be true of anything. So, assuming some E to which neither A nor B belongs, necessarily, he says, C and D will belong to it.[315]

But when he [sc. Aristotle] says that this E is intermediate between A and B, and argues that 'as they are contraries, what is neither [of them] must be intermediate [between them]', Alexander says that

> this, expressed thus *simpliciter*, is not true. For that to which the negations of both contraries apply is not necessarily intermediate, as has been shown.[316] However, [he says] he is not here talking of what is strictly speaking intermediate, but more generally he calls something intermediate between contraries if the negations of both hold true of it, insofar as it is identical to neither of them. Or he may have said this,

he says,

> elliptically instead of '[what is] neither of them completely is intermediate': for while it is not completely either of them, it still possesses something of each. And these are the kinds of things about which the argument is concerned. For that which neither always exists nor always does not exist participates to a certain extent both in that which always exists and in that which

always does not exist, of the one insofar as it exists at some time, of the other insofar as it does not exist at some time.

334,1

And that Aristotle does indeed take the concept of the intermediate in this way, as participating to a certain extent in both, he made clear when he said earlier that 'therefore the same thing will be capable of being, and capable of not being, and this is the intermediate between both [extremes]';[317] and he makes this even clearer in what comes before.[318]

5 Having undertaken to show that what exists always is neither generable nor destructible, and having shown that the negations of what always exists and what always fails to exist hold true of the generable and the destructible, which is the same thing, he infers as a reasonable conclusion that 'that which always exists is neither generable nor destructible, and similarly that which always does not exist'.

For if the contradictorily-opposed negation of always existing,
10 namely not always existing, holds of the generable and destructible, what always exists will be neither generable nor destructible, in order that the contradictory [predicates] will not be true at the same time of the same thing, namely the generable and destructible, with the affirmation which says it always exists being true (because of the supposition),[319] and the negation which says that it does not always exist being also true (because the negations of contraries must hold
15 true of the same thing).[320]

So from this the point of mentioning the contrary of always not existing becomes clear. The point was not to investigate something about this [as such], but rather, since what is generable and destructible was found to be intermediate between what always exists and what always does not exist, and since their negations held true of the same thing, it was for it to have been clearly shown that it is impossible for what always exists <and what does not always exist>[321]
20 to be at the same time generable or destructible.

282a22-5 And it is clear that if anything is either generable or destructible, [it will not be eternal; since it would be capable of always existing and capable of not always existing – and that this is impossible] has already been shown.

Having shown that what always exists is neither generable nor destructible, he goes on to show that these things convert, and that
25 neither the generable nor the destructible is eternal. For, he says, if the generable or the destructible is supposed to be eternal, the same thing will simultaneously be capable of being and not being, because (as Alexander says) that which always exists always exists and does not possess the capacity for at some time not existing, while the

generable and the destructible possess the capacity for at some time not existing.

So whenever it is supposed that what is capable of not existing at some time does not exist, it will not exist (by hypothesis), yet it will exist, because it is eternal.[322] And while the hypothesis which supposes that what is capable of not existing does not exist is false, it is not thereby impossible;[323] yet the conclusion, that the same thing is both existent and non-existent at the same time, is impossible: not, then, as a result of the hypothesis,[324] but as a result of positing the generable to be eternal. Thus Alexander was, I believe, paying attention to 'capable of not [always][325] being'.[326]

But if he says 'capable of being and capable of not being' in place of is and is not, as Alexander himself frequently indicated, then why do we not understand more simply that the same thing at some time both is and is not in respect of the same thing?[327] It exists, since it was established that it always existed, and it does not exist, since [in the case of] what is generable and destructible, just as it is at some time existent, so too at some time it is non-existent. For the fact that the 'capable of being' was said of that which always exists makes it plain that Aristotle does not say 'capable of not being' in the sense of something which is in actuality but is potentially non-existent, but rather that he posited it to stand for what does not exist.[328] For he could not mean in this case as well[329] that it was not in actuality, but was potentially, since what always is is in actuality. But 'capable' here does not mean potentially,[330] but rather possessing the capacity which goes along with the actuality. For this reason what is capable of being and what is capable of not being come to the same thing as what is and what is not.[331]

One might justly inquire, I think, why Aristotle should draw out so many arguments in aid of showing something really very self-evident. For what is more obvious than that what always exists is neither generable nor destructible, and again that what is generable and destructible does not always exist, given that what is generable and destructible is that which is capable of existing at some time and not existing at another? And which of the things which are assumed with a view to the demonstration of it are not more unclear than it is? So how could it not be absurd that Aristotle, the pre-eminent authority on such matters, could fail to see what was convincing in itself and unmediated,[332] and what needed the intermediate support of something else to be convincing?

Secondly one might inquire what need there is at all for him to provide a demonstration of this evident axiom. For what was at issue was to reply to those who thought it possible for something which was ungenerated to be destroyed, and for something that was generated to continue to be indestructible, as the *Timaeus* has it.[333] And it would have sufficed for this purpose to have expounded the conversion[334] of the generable and the destructible and of the ungenerable and the indestructible, which he goes on immediately to expound.

So perhaps now, in rebuttal of those who say that it [sc. the cosmos] is generated but indestructible, or ungenerated but destructible, he shows that these things cannot be combined with one another, given that he has shown what is ungenerable and what is indestructible are eternal, while what is generated and destructible is not eternal, having its being and non-being rather in a determinate time.[335]

He concludes in the second figure, with 'eternal' as the middle term, that it is possible neither that the ungenerated be destructible nor that the generated be indestructible.[336] So he shows not only that what is generated and destructible cannot be eternal (since that is really self-evident), but also what their nature is, and how they are related to what always exists, and that they are intermediate between what always is and what always is not, in that they participate partially in both of them. And from the fact that they are intermediate, [he shows] also that they follow from one another, which will be of use to him in showing that 'ungenerated' and 'indestructible'[337] follow from one another.

And having thus proved this proposition, which holds that what is generated and destructible does not exist for ever just as it is not always non-existent, he proceeds to show that the ungenerated and the indestructible always exist, by way of showing that they are reciprocally entailing, and this in turn by showing that 'generated' and 'destructible'[338] follow from one another.

282a25-30 So if something is indeed ungenerated and existent, [surely then it is of necessity eternal, and similarly if it is indestructible and existent? (I mean 'ungenerated' and 'indestructible' strictly speaking: 'ungenerated' means that which is existent now and for which it was not formerly true to say that it did not exist, while 'indestructible' means] that which is existent now, and for which it will not be true to say that it does not exist).

Having shown that what is eternal is neither generated nor destructible, from which it follows that what always exists is ungenerated and indestructible (for everything which exists is either generated or ungenerated and either destructible or indestructible), and having further shown that what is generated and destructible is not eternal, he next investigates whether the ungenerated and the indestructible are existent. He adds the word 'existent' to 'ungenerated' and 'indestructible', because, as these things are said in many ways, it is possible to predicate both 'ungenerated' and 'indestructible' both of that which is completely non-existent and of that which is not capable of coming to be,[338] such as that the diagonal[340] is commensurable with the side: for this non-existent is capable neither of coming to be nor of being destroyed.

Furthermore, being ungenerated and indestructible also holds true of that which exists at one time and fails to exist at another, but does not change from one to the other by any process of generation or destruction.[341] So, since these things are said in many ways, he distinguishes these latter from the non-existent [cases] by the addition of 'existent', and marks them off both from the non-existent and from any other sense they may have by the specification 'strictly speaking'. For now his main concern is with the account of what is strictly speaking meant by them.

However, although Alexander, when he sets out the passage, writes 'and similarly if it is indestructible and existent',[342] in his exegesis he expounds the passage as though it read 'and similarly if it is *eternal* and existent', and he says that 'ungenerated' is said also of that which is incapable of coming to be; for a diagonal's being commensurable with the side is ungenerated in this way, and it is possible to call this too eternal, since it is eternally incapable of being commensurable. 'He added "and existent" to each of them', he says, 'in order to mark off things called eternal and ungenerated in this sense from those things which are so called either because they are not and never will be, or in virtue of any of the other meanings it has.' But the texts of Aristotle which have come down to me are written as follows: 'and similarly if it is indestructible and existent'.[343] Moreover, the inquiry about whether what is both ungenerated and indestructible is eternal is concerned with both of them. For this reason he defined both of them as strictly speaking ungenerable and strictly speaking indestructible, in opposition to what is strictly generable and destructible: for by 'strictly speaking generable' he means that which now exists but is capable of previous non-existence, and by 'strictly speaking destructible' that which formerly existed, but is capable of later non-existence.

282a30-b7 Or, if these things follow from one another, [and it is the case both that the ungenerable is indestructible and the indestructible ungenerable, it follows necessarily that each of them is eternal, so that whatever is ungenerable is eternal, and whatever is indestructible is eternal. And this is clear from both of their definitions, since it is necessary that if it is destructible, it is generable, because it is either ungenerable or generable; but if it is ungenerable, it has been established that it is indestructible. But if it is generable, then it must be destructible; since it is either destructible or indestructible – but if indestructible it has been established that it is ungenerable. However, if indestructibility and ungenerability do not follow from one another, it is not necessary that] either the ungenerable or the indestructible should be eternal.

Having investigated whether being eternal follows from being ungenerable and indestructible, he now says that if these things follow from one another (in the sense that what is ungenerable is indestructible and what is indestructible ungenerable), necessarily being eternal will be implied by each of them. For what is ungenerable and at the same time indestructible, given that it is existent, is clearly eternal too. For it is capable neither of prior non-existence (given that it is ungenerable), nor of posterior [non-existence] (given that it is indestructible); while that for which it is never true to say that it does not exist, whether earlier or later, is necessarily eternal. So he rightly says that it is clear from the definition of 'ungenerable' and 'indestructible' that, as ungenerability and indestructibility follow from one another, eternality will follow from them too.

And he further indicates that if ungenerability and indestructibility follow from one another, necessarily generability and destructibility must follow from one another as well. For if it is not possible for what is destroyed to be generated, it will be ungenerable. But it was established that what was ungenerable was indestructible, so the destructible would be indestructible, which is impossible. And similarly, if something is generated, it must be destructible too, since if it is indestructible it is also ungenerated. But from[344] 'but if indestructible it has been established that it is ungenerable' he inferred[345] 'if it is generable, then it is necessarily destructible', omitting for brevity's sake the intermediate step 'since it is either destructible or indestructible'.[346]

Or does he rather infer as a consequence 'but if indestructible, it has been established that it is ungenerable'? But it would be remarkable, while setting out to show the [reciprocal] entailment of ungenerability and indestructibility by way of the [reciprocal] entailment of generability and destructibility, for him now to say that the [reciprocal] entailment of generability and destructibility follows from that of ungenerability and indestructibility.

But he appears to show by these means that whichever of these entailments obtains, necessarily the other will obtain as well. But if ungenerability and indestructibility do not follow from one another, it is not necessary, he says, for either the ungenerable or the indestructible to be eternal; for neither what is ungenerable but destructible nor what is indestructible but generable is capable of being eternal.

282b7-23 But that they must follow [from [one another] is evident from the following considerations. Generability and destructibility follow from one another; and this is clear from what was said earlier. For there is something between that which always exists and that which always does not, which entails neither of them, and this is what is generable and destructible, since each is capable both of existing and of not existing for a determinate time (I mean that each exists for a quantity of time, and does not exist [for a quantity of time]). So if there is anything either generable or destructible, it must be intermediate. Let A be what always exists, and B what always does not, C what is generable, and D what is destructible. C must then be between A and B, since there is no time for them in the direction of either limit in which either A does not exist or B does. For the generable, on the other hand, it is necessary that there be such a time either potentially or actually, but not for A or B in either way. Therefore there will be some determinate quantity of time for which it [sc. C] exists, and also in turn [some determinate quantity of time] for which it does not. And the same goes for D, the destructible.[347] Therefore each is both generable and destructible]. Therefore generability and destructibility follow from one another.

Having undertaken to show that ungenerability and indestructibility are reciprocally entailing, he does so on the basis of the reciprocal entailment of the generable and the destructible. For even if it is true that whichever of them you take to be reciprocally entailing, the others will be reciprocally entailing too, still the entailment of generability and destructibility seems to be more obvious, because of their being intermediate between what always exists and what always does not.

For having shown that the negations both of what always exists and of what always does not exist hold true of the same thing which is intermediate between both, and that this is what is capable of existing at one time and not existing at another, which is the generable and destructible, he infers that generability and destructibility follow from one another, given that they both hold of the same, single intermediate thing.[348]

So, reminding us now of this proof that generability and destructibility follow from one another, he says that it is clear from the earlier [premisses], which he now recalls, namely that intermediate between what always exists and what always does not there is that of which neither always existing nor always not existing holds. Thus it is necessary that their negations hold of it, given that in all cases it is necessary that either the affirmation or the negation be true.[349]

And that for which their negations holds is what is generable and destructible; for that which does not always exist and does not always not exist is capable both of being and not being, but neither of them always, given that in the phrases 'does not always exist' and 'does not always not exist', the 'always' is got rid of. So it is possible for both being and not being to hold of the intermediate for a determinate time, since [they do] not always [do so].³⁵⁰

For he says the same thing by the expression 'since each is capable both of being and of not being for a determinate time' as he does when he says 'for the negation of each will obtain at some time, if not always'.³⁵¹ For if it is neither capable of being always nor of not being always, each of them will obtain for it partially. So if there is anything at all which is in the nature of existing things which is generable and destructible, then the negations of the contraries will also hold of something which exists, i.e. what is intermediate, to which existence and non-existence belong serially, for some determinate time. He shows this once again by exposition by way of letters.

Letting A stand once again for what always exists, B for what always does not, C (which is the negation of A)³⁵² for what is generated, and D (which is the negation of B) for what is destructible, he shows first that the C (i.e. what is generated) is intermediate between what always exists and what always does not from the fact that there is no determinate time for either of the contraries, neither for what always exists nor for what always does not.

For by 'in the direction of neither limit' we should understand 'in the direction of neither the earlier nor the later'.³⁵³ For what always exists cannot fail to exist in any prior time, and nor can what always exists fail to exist in a later time. It is necessary that there be a certain determinate time, and a limit to the time of what is generated, in which it either exists or does not, in actuality or potentially. For it does not exist in actuality when, although generable, it has not yet been generated, and it exists in actuality when it has already been generated and exists. And potentially it does not exist because it has already been generated. For what already has been generated and exists has the potentiality for non-existence at an earlier time. For it existed potentially, prior to being generated.³⁵⁴

Similarly in the case of the destructible, these things can be seen to hold conversely. For it exists in actuality prior to being destroyed, and potentially after it has been destroyed, and does not exist in actuality when it has been destroyed, although it still exists potentially. For in general, what exists at one time and not at another, at all times is one of these things³⁵⁵ in actuality and the other potentially.³⁵⁶

Having said that in the case of the generated there must be a limit to the time in which it either exists or does not, in actuality or potentiality, he infers in the case of what always exists and what always does not (i.e. A and B) that it belongs in neither way to them to have a limit, to the one [a limit] of existence and to the other [a limit] of non-existence, either in actuality or potentially. That no limit of existence belongs in actuality to what always exists, or of non-existence to what always does not is clear, and that there is none potentially either you may understand from the fact that what they have potentially is capable of belonging to them at some time in actuality as well.

So if what always exists possesses potentially a limit of existence, while what always does not possesses potentially a limit of non-existence, then if one supposes that what they are capable of at some time belongs to them in actuality, what always exists will not exist and what always does not [exist] will exist, and consequently one thing will both exist and fail to exist in respect of the same thing, which is impossible, and not as a result of supposing that what exists in potentiality at some time becomes actual (for this was seen to be false, but not impossible too),[357] but insofar as[358] what is impossible follows from an impossibility.[359] And it followed that the same thing will both exist and not exist at the same time from the fact that non-existence belongs potentially to that which always exists, while existence [does potentially] to that which always does not.[360]

And discussing these things by way of a middle [term], he inferred the conclusion about the generable that 'therefore there will be some determinate quantity of time for which it [sc. C] exists, and also in turn [some determinate quantity of time] for which it does not'.[361] For it is established that the generable possesses a temporal limit, both for which it exists and for which it does not exist, either in actuality or potentially. And what he adds follows from this, namely that there is some determinate quantity of time both for its existence and for its non-existence: for a non-infinite time is determinate.[362]

From these [premisses] he infers that these things are congruent: for just as in the case of C, the generable, so to in the case of D, the destructible: this too must possess some temporal limit, and there must be a determinate time for its existence and non-existence. Then, by applying the same definition in both cases he inferred that 'therefore each is both generable and destructible', if indeed a determinate time belongs to each of them for their existence and their non-existence. And if it is the case that what is generable is destructible and what is destructible is generable, and the same formula applies to both, the generable and the destructible are reciprocally entailing, which is what he proposed to show.

These things have already been shown earlier, when he showed that negations of the contraries of always existing and always not existing hold true of the same thing.[363] But one should not suppose that this holds in general, namely that if intermediate between certain things are others, to which the negations of the contraries hold true, then they are reciprocally entailing; for it is not true to say this. Yellow and red are intermediate between white and black (which are contraries), and the negations of the contraries (i.e. of white and black) hold true for each of them, but they do not follow from one another.³⁶⁴

30 But that there is something which is at all events intermediate between them, to which the negation of each applies, is as it were a property of these contraries (i.e. of always existing and always not existing). For the same does not hold in general for the other contraries, be they either with or without intermediates. And in this way the fact that their intermediates follow from one another is a property of
341,1 them. For in that things intermediate between them, which participate in each of them to a certain extent, at one time exist and at another time do not, and [in that] each of these (namely existence and non-existence) [holds of them] for a determinate time, there is a single formula for them. And those things for which the formula is one and the same are the same as each other and differ in name only, as Alexander says. Consequently they will reciprocally entail one an-
5 other, since they are the same.³⁶⁵

'That their formula is the same', he says,

> is clear from the fact that each of them possesses the capacity both for existing and for not existing; and it has been shown that everything which possesses the capacity for existing and not existing possesses the capacity for each of them for a determinate time. For it is not possible to possess the capacity both for existing and for not existing to infinity. Consequently each of
> 10 them will in turn be generated and destroyed.

Having said these things, Alexander notes that perhaps what he [sc. Aristotle] has said so far about the proof that the generable and the destructible reciprocally entail one another will not seem sufficient; for their definitions are not the same. For while the possibility of not being at some time is common to both of them, it is not the *same* time
15 in both cases. For one of them indicates an earlier time, the other a later one.³⁶⁶ And it is not necessary from what has been established that what is capable of not being earlier is also capable of not being later. 'Moreover', he says, 'even in the case of the yellow and the red it is true to say that they participate in each of the contraries of white and black to a certain extent; but they do not for this reason immediately follow from one another'.

20 Having rightly drawn attention to these things, he concludes that the strength of the argument depends for Aristotle on the fact that the generable and the destructible possess for a time determinate in both directions³⁶⁷ the capacity for being and not being. And this in turn depends upon the negations³⁶⁸ being true of them. For it is clear that what is such as not always to exist has the capacity for being for
25 a determinate and limited time, since for this reason it is not true of

it that it always exists. Therefore, because it changes from existing to not existing it is destructible, given that it does not always exist.

On the other hand, what does not exist in such a way as not always, but only at some times, not to exist, must also advance into existence, given that it is not always non-existent. Therefore what changes from non-existence to existence is generable. So if the negations are true of the same thing,[369] the one ('not always existent') signifying the destructible and the other ('not always non-existent') the generable,[370] then the latter, i.e. the generable, is also destructible, and [the former], the destructible, is also generable, and they follow from one another, each of them having for some determinate time the capacity both for being and for not being.

And it was also shown earlier that what is generable must necessarily be destructible. For if it has been generated, since what is generated is generated from something existent and generation is a kind of change, then it comes to be this from having had the capacity.[371] Therefore, having changed into this, it will possess the capacity for changing back into that from which this came to be.[372] For in fact it changes into this while preserving its proper nature, which was the capacity to admit contraries in turn. So if what has been generated changes again, it will be destroyed, and being destructible will follow from being generable. On the other hand, what is destructible will possess the capacity for being as it was prior to its being destroyed and having been destroyed. Therefore when it was destroyed, that into which it was destroyed will possess the capacity for changing back into its contrary, from which it also came to be.[373] Consequently being generable will reciprocally entail being destructible.

So, are these confirmations sufficient in regard to the convertibility of the generable and the destructible? Or is it possible to say in regard to the argument from the negations that these negations (i.e. not always existing and not always not existing) apply not only to what is generable and destructible, but also to what is generable but indestructible? In fact, this too does not exist always, because it advanced into being from prior non-existence, and thus exists as generable, and is not always non-existent, given that it is indestructible and will continue infinitely in being for the rest of time.[374]

But Alexander, while apparently granting this difficulty, takes refuge rather in the other demonstration of the reciprocal entailment of the generable and destructible, which says that it follows for that which is intermediate that it possesses a capacity not for an infinite [time][375] of existence and non-existence, but only for a determinate one. And if this is the case, that which is capable of coming to be will have a determinate period of time for which it is capable of not existing, and that which is generated from it in turn will possess the capacity for existing for a determinate time, and what is generable in this way changes in turn in the direction of non-existence.[376] And so what is generable will be destructible too.

But perhaps it is also possible to resolve the difficulty by saying that not always existing does not hold true of that which is generated but indestructible. For if the indestructible is what has being to an infinite extent for the rest of time, and what is to an infinite extent is something which exists always, it will be true to say of it that it always exists, even if the 'always' only holds in one direction.[377]

However, in regard to the second demonstration of the fact that generability and destructibility reciprocally entail one another, the one based on the fact that each has a determinate time of being and not being, Alexander himself rightly raises difficulties.

'For one might inquire', he says,

what is meant by 'therefore there will be some determinate quantity of time for which it [sc. C] exists, and also in turn [some determinate quantity of time] for which it does not'.[378] For while it appears that there will be some determinate time for the existence of everything in [the realm of] generation, it no longer [seems so] for their non-existence. For in the case of the simples, change is indeed from determinate and contrary things to determinate and contrary things, for instance from hot to cold and *vice versa*, and in other cases equally there would be a determinate time for both this fire[379] and this water, [a time] in which each of them both is and is not. But in the case of composites like plants and animals, while there is a determinate time for their existence, there is not for their non-existence. For when any of them is destroyed, it is non-existent for the infinite remainder of time, just as was the case prior to its generation; for during that time too, which was infinite, it did not exist. Thus Socrates, having perished, does not possess the capacity of non-existence for a determinate time, given that he will necessarily not be generated again.[380] And in general,

he says,

in cases where the underlying matter can change into many things and not only into a single thing, as we see in the case of the matter underlying animals and plants, how can the time for each thing's non-existence be determinate in these cases, at least if what underlies them is capable of changing into different things at different times, and for this reason will never again recur as the man?[381]

Having set out these difficulties he concludes that, with regard to showing that the same thing is at the same time both generable and destructible (which is the point at issue), it is enough [to show] that each of the things subject to generation and destruction has a determinate time for its existence, even if the time of its non-existence is not determinate; for if the time of existence for the non-eternal things is determinate in both directions, so that it has both a beginning and an end, they will be both generated and destroyed. But why did Aristotle not think that the determinate time of existence for things subject to generation sufficed for the generable and the destructible to follow from one another, but posited in addition that for a determinate time they did not exist?

'He would have posited this', Alexander says,

> not in the belief that the time of their future existence and their future non-existence was determinate in the same way, but in the belief that while [the time] of their future existence is strictly speaking determinate,[382] that of their future non-existence is also automatically determinate in that it is not infinite. For he calls it determinate, opposing it to the infinite. For the time for which each thing does not exist is determined by the time in which it exists, and its infinitude is destroyed. So the time of non-existence is determinate in this way, namely that it is not infinite.[383]

It is also possible to speak of the time of non-existence as determinate in the sense that it has some measurable quantity, just as that of existence: for this is clear in the case of the simple bodies. For the time for each of the things in which change occurs in the substrate is determinate, given that the change is from something contrary and determinate into something contrary and determinate; for the intermediates are in a way contraries.[384]

In the case of composites like plants and animals, the simple bodies out of which each of them is [composed] will exist and not exist for a determinate time on account of their changing into their contraries in turn; but they are not prevented from coming to be again in the same form. For while it is not possible for numerically the same individual to be preserved in such cases, it is not impossible that the things from which it was [composed] should, after its destruction, change once again to receive that form, so that the elements of a horse should, after the destruction of the horse, change into the elements of wasps and take on the form of wasps,[385] and then, after that has been destroyed, change into the elements of a horse and take on the form of a horse, either immediately or after being other things in the interim.

Not that in actuality it will necessarily be this thing once again, as Alexander says, because of the capacity that the things of which the horse was composed have for coming to be other things and not once again a horse. However it is impossible for something of this kind to be eternal because the things of which they are composed necessarily have the capacity for changing. But perhaps since generation goes on infinitely, it is necessary that numerically the same matter will once again receive the same forms, and the body [will too], given that it too is eternal.[386]

And it is not at all surprising that the four elements which directly underlie the composite forms should remain numerically the same (e.g. this fire and this water, even if it were to adopt some other disposition prior to changing into contraries), and if they are disposed and fitted together in the same way again that they should become receptive of the same forms of animal or plant. Consequently it is true in the case of the composites too that they have a determinate time not only for their existence but also for their non-existence, if the elements are the same even numerically, and the composites evidently recur [that are the same] in form.[387]

282b23-283a4 Now let E be the ungenerable, [F the generable, G the indestructible, and H the destructible. It has been demonstrated that F and H follow from one another. But whenever things are related in this way, such that F and H follow from one another while E and F can never belong to the same thing, but everything is either one or the other and the same is true of G and H, then E and G must also follow from one another. For suppose E does not follow from G: F must then follow from it, since everything is either E or F. But whatever is F is also H; therefore H will follow from G; but it has been established that this is impossible. And the same argument establishes that G follows from E. Furthermore, the same relation holds between the ungenerable (i.e. E) and the generable (i.e. F)] as between the indestructible (i.e. G) and the destructible (i.e. H).

Having undertaken to show that both the ungenerable and the indestructible are eternal, he says that this can be shown in no other way than by showing that the ungenerable and the indestructible are reciprocally entailing with one another, and this only by showing that the generable and the destructible are reciprocally entailing with one another.[388]

So having shown this, he relies on it to prove next that the ungenerable and the indestructible reciprocally entail one another. And he proves this by way of the following general theorem. Suppose we take two terms which stand in a relation of contradictory opposition to one another, so that while both cannot belong to the same thing, one of them must necessarily belong to anything you care to suppose. 'Generable' and 'ungenerable' stand in this relation,[389] for even if they are not contradictorily opposed (because the ungenerable is a positive attribute too),[390] even so there is nothing to which they can both belong, since it is impossible for the same thing to be both generable and ungenerable. And one of them must necessarily belong to anything you care to suppose, since it is necessary that everything that exists is either generable or ungenerable.

Assume further two other terms which are related in the same way as they are, namely 'destructible' and 'indestructible': there is nothing to which these can both belong either, although one of them must belong to anything. And one of the second pair follows from one of the first, while the other follows from the other. He showed that this was the case also in the second book of the *Prior Analytics*;[391] and he now proves it by *reductio ad impossibile*, generating a general demonstration using letters in following way.

He assigns E to the ungenerable, F to the generable, G to the indestructible, and H to the destructible. So since the generable and the destructible (i.e. F and H) have been shown to follow from one another,[392] I say that the others too are reciprocally entailing, and that E and G will belong to the same thing, that is to say both the ungenerable and the indestructible: for if E does not follow from G (i.e. the ungenerable from the indestructible),[393] F must follow from G; for either E or F must belong to everything, hence the generable will follow from the indestructible.[394] But it has been shown that F and H (that is to say the generable and the destructible) follow from one another. Consequently H, the destructible, will follow from[395] G (that is to say the indestructible), which is impossible: for it was established that G and H were so related to one another that there was nothing to which both could belong.[396]

But the destructible and the indestructible do stand in this relation to one another, since it is impossible for the same thing to be both destructible and indestructible. So if when we suppose that E does not follow from G (i.e. the ungenerable from the indestructible), something impossible results, namely that the same thing is at the same time both destructible and indestructible, it is clear that what was posited[397] is impossible. Therefore E will follow from G, i.e. the ungenerable from the indestructible.

And because of the same necessary implication, G will follow from E, i.e. the indestructible from the ungenerable. For if this were not the case, H, i.e. the destructible, [would do so], since one or the other must do so. But F has been shown to follow from H, i.e. the generable from the destructible; and therefore F will follow from E[398] as well, and the same thing will be at the same time generable and ungenerable, which is impossible. Therefore the indestructible follows from the ungenerable; and consequently the eternal [follows] from both of them. For it is clear that what is at the same time both ungenerable and indestructible is eternal, since it has neither a beginning for its existence (since it is ungenerable), nor an end (since it is indestructible). So if the generable and destructible have their existence in a part of time and are not eternal, it will be possible neither for something generable to be indestructible, nor for something ungenerable to be destructible, for otherwise the same thing would be both eternal and non-eternal.

And so, with the eternal as the middle term, he lays out the whole demonstration that nothing ungenerable can be destructible, and nor can anything generable be indestructible;[399] and what he has already demonstrated in the case of the heaven by physical arguments, when he showed it to be ungenerated and indestructible from the fact that it has no contrary,[400] he now sets out to examine the question in general terms, since the general demonstration that there is nothing ungenerable which is destructible and nothing generable which is indestructible applies in the case of the heaven too.

283a4-10 So to say that there is nothing to prevent [something generated from being indestructible, and something ungenerable from being destroyed, as though the coming to be of one and the destruction of the other occurred once only, is to destroy one of the things which have been granted. For everything which is capable of acting or being acted upon, or of being or not being, is so either for an infinite or for some determinate quantity of time; and for an infinite time only for this reason, namely that the infinite time is in a sense determinate, that than which there is no greater.] The infinite in one direction only is neither infinite nor determinate.

He has shown that the generable and the destructible (and equally the ungenerable and the indestructible) are reciprocally entailing, and that the indestructible, being eternal, cannot be generable, and equally that the ungenerable, being eternal (given that it is also indestructible), cannot be destructible. Now he finally confronts those who think that nothing prevents one from saying that the same thing can be generable and at the same time indestructible, as Plato apparently clearly says that the world was both generated by the Demiurge, and that it will never be destroyed: 'to wish to destroy something well fitted-together and happy', he says, 'is the work of evil'.[401]

No one apparently says that it can be ungenerated and at the same time destructible, although Aristotle destroys this hypothesis too in his refutations, by parity of reasoning. However Alexander attributes this [hypothesis] too to Plato on the basis of [the following] argument: 'for it follows', he says, 'that someone who says that what is generated is indestructible must also say that what is ungenerated is destructible'.[402]

First he [sc. Aristotle] adduces against those who say these things that they destroy one of the things which have been granted; and it is clearly absurd to destroy what has been granted.⁴⁰³ But what is this thing, which was granted and demonstrated, and which [is it which] those who say this destroy? Alexander says that it is the reciprocal entailment of the generable and the destructible and the ungenerable and the indestructible. For these things, which have already been shown, are destroyed by those who say that the generable is indestructible or the ungenerable destructible. And he [sc. Alexander] supposed that Aristotle speaks in what follows of certain other destroyed [suppositions] when he says 'for everything which is capable of acting or being acted upon ... is so either for an infinite or for some determinate quantity of time'.

But Alexander gets rid of the causal connective 'for',⁴⁰⁴ which clearly connects the supposition which is destroyed by those who speak in this way, to no purpose. For if it is assumed and agreed that the things which act or are acted upon in time (for those beyond time are outside the scope of the argument) act or are acted upon either in an infinite or in a determinate time.⁴⁰⁵ For it is necessary to act or be acted upon, or to exist or not exist, in a time which is determinate in some way; and while strictly speaking a determinate time is one which has a beginning and an end, infinite time is also conceptually determinate, in that it always is, as Alexander says,⁴⁰⁶ and in that there is nothing outside it.⁴⁰⁷

And it is not necessary to assume as infinite the time which is actually infinite, but only the one which tends towards the infinite.⁴⁰⁸ For time infinite in actuality does not exist, but only that which is considered to tend towards infinity. This is the infinite which Aristotle says is 'that than which there is no greater'. For there is no other time greater than that which tends towards infinity, since there is no infinity of time in actuality, or indeed in general any infinity of this sort, as was shown in Book 3 of the *Physics*.⁴⁰⁹

However, in the case of the time which tends towards infinity, even if it [goes on] for ever, there will always be a time beyond what has been taken;⁴¹⁰ but this is a part of it [sc. the infinite], and there is nothing outside this whole, just as there is no time greater than it. And this is the infinite time, which is infinite and determined in the direction of the infinite, and by the fact that it is uninterrupted and that there is nothing greater than it.

But the infinite in one direction only,⁴¹¹ for example what is generated but indestructible, or ungenerated but destructible, is determinate in no way, neither in having a beginning and end (as the limited does), nor in having nothing greater than it (as the infinite does). For there is more time beyond each of them (although not in each direction), of the generated but indestructible before it exists, and of the ungenerated but destructible after it exists.

'At the same time', Alexander says,

he resolves an objection which could be brought against the established entailment of the generable and the destructible. For if the reason why they follow from one another is that for both of them their time both of existence and non-existence is determinate, and if for the generated but indestructible non-existence is determinate in respect of the beginning while existence is so in respect of the end, while the opposite holds for the ungenerated but destructible, it is not necessary that things which exist for a determinate time should follow from one another. So he resolves this objection,

he says,

by means of [the argument that] whatever acts or is acted upon, or exists or does not exist, must do so in a determinate time, while that which is infinite in one direction only is determinate neither as being limited in each direction nor as being unexceeded.

283a11-17 Further, what more reason is there at this point [[rather than any other] why something which had previously existed for ever should be destroyed, or why something which was non-existent for an infinite time should be generated? For if there is no more reason why, and the points extend infinitely, it is clear that something generable or destructible will exist for an infinite time. Therefore it is capable of not existing for an infinite time (for it will have at the same time the capacity for not existing and for existing), in the case of the destructible beforehand, and in the case of the generable afterwards]. Consequently if we suppose that its capacities are realised, the opposites will obtain simultaneously.

He has shown that anyone who says that there is something generated but indestructible, or ungenerated but destructible, destroys one of the things established and granted, namely that things which either act or are acted upon in time either act or are acted upon (or exist or fail to exist) either in an infinite or in a limited time. For what is generated but indestructible, and what is ungenerated but destructible, have their existence and non-existence neither in an infinite[412] nor in a limited time.

So, having shown this, he also shows by way of another argument that people who say this get rid of something [generally] agreed, namely that it is impossible for something both to be and not to be at the same time; for it is agreed that this is impossible, and this impossibility results for them, given that they say that something which they suppose to be ungenerated (i.e. to have existed for all previous time) is at some time destroyed.

For since there are an infinite number of nows[413] in the infinite time in which the ungenerated formerly existed, it either possesses the capacity for being destroyed in all those nows equally, or in some distinct one. But the latter is plainly absurd; for what reason could there be for something which has lasted an infinite time before this to be destroyed in this now rather than that?[414]

For this reason Aristotle, having pointed this out by way of [the clause] 'what more reason is there at this point [rather than any other] why something which had previously existed for ever be destroyed', turns to the other disjunct, namely that it possesses the capacity for being destroyed in all those nows equally, given that it does not do so in this one rather than that. And since the nows are infinite, the ungenerated object will have possessed the capacity for being destroyed and not existing for the infinite time prior to this one during which it was in existence. So what is ungenerated but destructible will possess, at the same time as being in actuality, the capacity for not being, and consequently if we assume that what is possible obtains,[415] what is ungenerated will be non-existent; and so at the same time it will be existent and non-existent, which is impossible.

And similarly, what is generable but non-existent for an infinite prior time will not have possessed the capacity for coming to be in this now any more than that one, but in all of them similarly. So too in this case, whenever we posit that what is possible [for this thing] obtains [for it], since it possesses the capacity for existing even though it does not exist in actuality, the same thing will be at the same time non-existent and existent, which is similarly impossible.

So if to suppose that something which is possible obtains is false but not impossible,[416] while it is not just false but impossible that the same thing should at the same time both exist and not exist (or not exist and exist),[417] it is clear that an impossibility followed not from supposing that something obtains which is possible (which was false but not impossible), but from [the supposition] of its possessing the capacity for the opposite for an infinite prior time; and this is impossible.[418] So it is impossible for something to be generated but indestructible or ungenerated but destructible, given that these things must possess the capacity for the opposite for an infinite prior time.

And this is the subject[419] of the entire argument. In the phrase 'or why something which was non-existent for an infinite ... should be generated' Alexander says the expression is elliptical: for the whole phrase should read 'something which was non existent for an infinite *time* should be generated'.[420] But perhaps 'infinite' said adverbially in the sense of 'to infinity' is not an ellipsis.[421] That in which things have been destroyed or generated he calls 'points',[422] because while destruction and generation [take place] in time, to have been destroyed or generated are timeless and in the now, as was shown in the treatise the *Physics*.[423]

But although everywhere else he posits the two [possibilities], namely of something ungenerated but destructible and of something generated but indestructible, in posing the argument briefly, Aristotle creates an unclarity in the phrase 'therefore it is capable of not existing for an infinite time' by not adding 'and also existing', which holds true of what is generated but indestructible. But he omitted it for brevity's sake as being evident, and understood from the other case.[424]

283a17-20 Moreover, this will obtain equally at every point, [and thus it will have the capacity both for existing and for not existing for an infinite time]. But it has been shown that this is impossible.

Alexander says: 'this would have been expressed more clearly if instead of this he had written "this will obtain equally at every time", since he does not show this now, but assumes it as something which follows from what has already been shown'.

But perhaps although this is presented as following from what has been said, he draws a further, even more absurd conclusion from it, that not only will it have to exist and not exist at the same time in some part of time,[425] but that this result will hold for the whole infinity of time. For it has the capacity for existing and not existing in every now of the infinite time, in the one case having the actuality along with the capacity, in the other the capacity only.[426] For it has it no more in one now than in any other.[427]

So whenever one supposes that what is possible obtains for it, it will at the same time possess existence and non-existence throughout the infinity of time. Thus it sufficed for Aristotle for it to possess the capacity for existence and non-existence for an infinite time, since it follows from this that it both exists and does not exist for the infinity of time in actuality too, whenever we suppose that what is possible for it obtains.

283a20-4 And again, if the potentiality obtains prior to the actuality, [it will obtain for all time, even when it was ungenerated and did not exist <for an infinite time>[428] but was capable of coming to be; thus for all the time it did not exist it did have the capacity for existing, both then and later;] and therefore for an infinite time.

He shows the same thing by way of this argument too, namely that if one supposes something can be generated and indestructible, it must possess the capacity for existing and not existing for an infinite time (this follows from its actually existing and not existing for an infinite time, which he omitted as being obvious). And he shows that it has the capacity for existing and not existing for an infinite time by assuming as obvious that where the potentiality and the actuality apply to the same thing, as for instance that of existing and of not existing, in these cases at all events what exists potentially precedes what exists in actuality, and such a potentiality [precedes] the actuality.[429] For by 'potentially' we mean that which is capable of being brought into actuality.[430]

So the generable, for that infinite time[431] prior to its being generated in which it was thus far ungenerated (for he cited this as a sense of 'ungenerable'),[432] possessed the capacity for being generated. And it possesses it also when it has already been generated, since what has been generated is capable of existing and of having been generated, but here the capacity does not exist prior to the actuality. So it will also have the capacity for existing in all of the infinite time prior to its generation, in which it did not yet exist. For at the time it did not exist it possessed the capacity both for existing and for being generated, even though it was thus far ungenerated. And this capacity will hold for it when it has been generated too, i.e. when it is no longer actually ungenerated, as Aristotle briefly indicates with 'it will obtain for all time, even when it was ungenerated and did not exist', meaning 'and when it is no longer ungenerated, but already generated'.[433]

And thus it has the capacity in such a way as to be capable of coming to be for an infinite time, given that even when it exists it is capable of existing; and while it does not exist it has the capacity not only of not existing, but of existing both earlier and later: i.e. of existing always *simpliciter*. For what would be the reason why something which did not exist for an infinite time came to be and existed at the time when it is said to, rather than earlier or later? Therefore it possesses the capacity for existing and not existing for an infinite time, from which it follows that whenever what is possible is brought to actuality, it will both exist and not exist for an infinite time. That what did not exist for an infinite prior time possessed the capacity for an infinite time of existing is clear, if indeed there is no necessity for its coming to be at that time rather than earlier or later.[434]

'He drew this conclusion', Alexander says, 'in the case of the generable, and will then immediately go on to draw it in the case of the destructible'. Perhaps, however, as he himself evidently understood, this proof applies to both of them,[435] while the succeeding argument[436] looks towards something different. For just as that which is generated but indestructible possesses the capacity for existing to an infinite extent even prior to its generation when it does not exist, so too that which is ungenerated but at the same time destructible possesses the capacity for not existing while it exists.

283a24-9 It is also evident for other reasons [that it is impossible for something which is destructible not to be destroyed at some time; for it will both always exist and at the same time be destructible <and indestructible>[437] in reality; so at the same time it would have the capacity for always existing and for not always existing. Therefore the destructible will at some time be destroyed; and if it is generable, then it will have come into being, since it is capable of having come to be,] and so therefore [it is capable] of not always existing.

When Plato says in the *Timaeus* 'everything bound together may be dissolved, but to wish to destroy something well fitted-together and happy is the work of evil',[438] and again in the voice of the Demiurge to the heavenly gods: 'you are not altogether immortal, but you will not be dissolved, nor will you happen upon the destiny of death',[439] he seems apparently to say that the world, although dissoluble, mortal and destructible in its own nature, will not be destroyed.

So Aristotle, in reply to the apparent thrust of the argument, says 'it is evident ... that it is impossible for something which is destructible' – i.e. in its own nature – 'not to be destroyed at some time'. And if this is the case, at the same time as it will always be (i.e. it will be eternal), it will also be destructible, and [it will be] both in reality (i.e. both in actuality), and not only potentially destructible, but in such a way that it will both be eternal and have been destroyed, which is plainly absurd. For if it is absurd for the eternal to be destructible merely in the sense that it is of a nature to be destroyed (because that for which it has a nature must at some time be brought to actuality), the absurdity will be all the more obvious when it is considered to be both in actuality: for while the same thing may possess the capacity for opposites as long as it does not do so eternally, it is impossible for it to possess the actualities at the same time. So he justifiably added 'in reality'.

Alexander thinks that the text should rather be transposed as follows: 'it will always exist in reality, while at the same time being destructible'. 'For this', he says,

is what seems rather to be made clear by the passage. For if it will always exist in reality, although being destructible, it will have the capacity of always existing, because it does in fact exist always, but also that of not always existing, since it is supposed to be destructible. For the destructible is that which has the capacity of not always existing, or of at some time not existing.

So it will thus at some time have the power of both existing and not existing at the same time.

However, perhaps 'for it will be eternal at the same time as being destructible in reality' would be clearer, from which it follows that it will at the same time always exist and not always exist, which is to make [both sides of] a contradiction be true at the same time. Again, he posited the capacity as being common both to what exists actually and to what exists potentially; for what is acting is also capable [of acting].[440]

'He writes', Alexander says,

> the following: 'for it will always exist and at the same time will also be destructible in reality'.[441] And this is the sense of what is said: if something which is destructible is never actually destroyed, it would always exist, i.e. it would be eternal and indestructible; and if this is the case it will possess the capacity for always existing (since it always is in actuality), but (since it is destructible) it will be capable of not always existing; for this is what being destructible is. Therefore it will at the same time be capable both of always existing and not always existing, which is impossible.[442] And if the passage has this sense,

he says,

> he leaves us to supply 'and indestructible', so the whole would read 'for it will always exist and at the same time will also be both indestructible and destructible in reality'.[443]

And I have come across a text which has it thus.

Having shown that it is impossible for something destructible by nature to be indestructible, he concluded 'therefore the destructible will at some time be destroyed'. 'And so', Alexander says, 'the world too, insofar[444] as it is destructible in its own nature (since it is generated), will not be eternal, but will at some time be destroyed'.

But that Aristotle opposes the appearance of Plato's doctrines rather than their genuine sense is clear, as I said before,[445] given that Plato does not mean that the world was generated at some particular time, since he says that time was generated along with the heaven,[446] and that there is a time which exists prior to the generation of anything that is generated at some particular time. Rather he says that the world is generated in the sense that it is perceptible and corporeal, and a descendant of what is really real, since it has its being in becoming.[447]

He calls what is 'bound together' and 'not altogether immortal' generable in its own nature in the same way as Aristotle showed that a limited body possesses a capacity limited in its own nature.[448] Both Plato and Aristotle demonstrated that the world was indestructible and immortal through God's immediate provision, the former by saying in the voice of the Demiurge: 'but you will not be dissolved, nor will you happen upon the destiny of death, since you derive from my will a greater and more powerful bond than these',[449] the latter because the immobile cause causes that which is directly moved by it to move eternally, even if the latter possesses a limited capacity, since it is limited by its own nature.[450]

Having concluded that what is destructible must at some time be destroyed, he concluded 'and if it is generable, then it will have come into being', not in the manner of someone who says that the world is generable although it will never come to be, unless, Alexander says, those who call what is not in fact destroyed 'destructible' say that it is generable although it will not come to be. For that into which the world, being destructible, would change is generable although it will never come to be, given that what ought to change into it is never destroyed.[451]

But having shown that the destructible cannot fail to be destroyed, he infers as a corollary of this that what is generable must come to be by a similar consequence. And this can be adduced in confirmation of the fact that the destructible will be destroyed. For in the same way as someone who calls something generable says that it will at some time be generated, so too someone calling something destructible will agree that it will be destroyed.

And in line with this conception, says Alexander, he inferred 'and so therefore of not always existing'. For not always existing applies to the destructible, and is capable of belonging to the generable, since it is true to say of this too, if it formerly did not exist but later does, that it does not exist always. And it was said earlier[452] that both negations apply to both the generable and the destructible, namely both 'not always existent' and 'not always non-existent', from which it was shown that the generable and the destructible convert with one another, being distinguished [from everything else] as according to a single nature intermediate between what always exists and what always fails to exist.

283a29-b6 It can also be seen in the following manner [that it is impossible both for something which has at some time come to be to continue as indestructible, and for something that is ungenerated and has always previously existed to be destroyed. For nothing can be either undestroyed or ungenerated by chance, since chance and lucky outcomes are the opposite of what either always or for the most part either is or comes to be. But that which is for an infinite time, whether *simpliciter* or from a certain point, obtains either always, or for the most part. Therefore it must be by nature that such things are at some times and not at others. In things of this kind, the capacity for opposites is the same, and the material is the cause both of being and of not being. Consequently] opposite states would have to obtain in actuality at the same time.

In answer to those who apparently maintain the world is destructible in its own nature and yet is not destroyed, and by parity of reasoning that it is generable but never exists, he returns once again to the same notion,[453] showing that it is impossible for something generated to continue as indestructible, or something ungenerated and existent for the whole of previous time to be destroyed. The demonstration is in a way similar to the one offered earlier, but in a way different. It goes as follows.

The generated but indestructible or ungenerated but destructible are either so by nature, or by chance, or by luck.[454] This disjunction is exhaustive[455] in the case of things which require a cause for their existence, and both what is generated and what is destroyed are of such a kind. But everything [that occurs] by luck or chance is always rare, and neither always nor for the most part,[456] while the ungenerated and the indestructible exist for an infinite time, whether they co-exist with each other for a time that is infinite in both directions (i.e. one which has neither beginning nor end, but is infinite *simpliciter*), or (if one supposes something ungenerated but destructible or generated but indestructible), a time which is infinite in one direction and which [starts] from some point.

And it is clear that the things which either exist or do not exist infinitely in both directions either always exist or always fail to exist, while those that do so in one direction do so for the most part.[457] So if things of this sort either exist or fail to exist either always or for the most part, while those that do so by chance or luck do so neither always nor for the most part, it follows in the second figure[458] that nothing generated but indestructible or ungenerated but destructible can exist either by luck or by chance.

So these things are necessarily such by nature, their existence at one time and their non-existence at another, since they have in one direction either everlasting existence or everlasting non-existence. But as nature remains the same, so too the capacity remains the same, as does the substrate, since it possesses the same capacity, and does not lose it in changing into the contraries, given that the matter is eternal. So, since both the nature and the matter remain the same, the same capacity must exist for ever.[459]

For prior to its becoming fire or one of the other elements, the matter possessed the capacity for becoming these things, and having done so it has not lost these capacities, but persists in having the

355,1 same ones. For the same matter has the capacity both for being something concrete and for not being it (for this is what it is to be matter for it), and is indestructible. For what could it be destroyed into? So if something generated, prior to its generation, possesses the capacity for not being this thing which it will become, it will persist in having the same capacity after its generation.

5 So if the world is supposed to be generated but indestructible, then after its generation it will have the capacity for not existing: for there was a time when it did not. So if it is supposed to be indestructible, and will exist for the rest of eternity possessing in actuality the capacity for not being, then whenever we suppose that what is possible [obtains], it will at the same time both exist and not exist in actuality. Consequently opposites will belong to the same thing at the

10 same time, which is impossible and follows from an impossibility: not the supposition of what was possible (for this was not impossible, but rather it is necessary that what is in something eternal potentially be at some time brought to actuality), but the supposition that something eternal possesses at the same time the capacity for not being at some time.

Similarly what was destroyed possesses the capacity for once again coming to be what it was previously, since the substrate is eternal and
15 always possesses the capacities for being and not being any of the composites.

> **283b6-14** Furthermore, it is not true to say [of something now that it exists[460] last year, or of something last year that it exists now. Therefore it is impossible for something which at one time was not later to become eternal. For it will have later the capacity of not existing (not at any rate of not-existing-when-it-does-exist – since then it is in actuality – but last year or in time past). Suppose then that what it has the capacity for actually obtains: therefore it will be true to say now that it does not exist last year. But that is impossible, since no capacity is for having come to be,] but only for what is and what will be.

Having shown that it follows for whoever maintains that something generated can be indestructible that it has the capacity for opposites
20 to belong to it at the same time, he goes on to resolve the following objection which could be brought against the argument. What is generable but indestructible has the capacity for not existing in respect of the past, given that it exists later having formerly not existed, and [the capacity] for existing in the future, given that it is posited as being indestructible. Therefore it will not possess the capacity for existing and not existing at the same time, and consequently will not possess opposite [properties] at the same time in actuality.

He resolves this objection by saying that every capacity is either for the present or for the future.[461] For we say that things are potential in the strict sense if they do not yet exist but can come to be, differentiating them in this way from things which exist, in that they will be but are not yet. So if it is not true of anything 'to say ... now that it exists last year' (or that it does not exist last year: for both are written),[462] since it is not true now to say that last year exists, it will not be true to say of any of the things which were last year that they are now; but nor was it true last year to say that the present part of time, which has come to be after a year, existed. For it is not possible to swap around the times.[463]

So if this is true, it will be impossible for what does not exist at some time later to be eternal, i.e. for something generated to become indestructible for the remainder [of time]. For since it exists later having formerly not existed, it will possess the capacity for non-existence even when it has been generated, but not of not-existing-at-that-time, when it has already been generated. For it exists in actuality when it exists at that time.[464] So such a thing must have possessed this capacity a year ago, that is, in time past.[465]

And although this is absurd, given that no capacity is for having come to be in the past but for being [now] or for being in the future, he adds by way of greater clarification 'suppose then that what it has the capacity for actually obtains: therefore it will be true to say now' concerning that which now possesses the capacity for not existing, not only that it possessed the capacity for not existing a year ago, but also 'that it does not exist last year'; which is something even more absurd, namely that it now exists in its not existing a year ago. For a year ago will exist now, since it is now posited to possess the capacity for not existing a year ago.[466]

Observe, then, that the more appropriate reading is 'that it is not last year':[467] and in fact this is what he concluded when he said 'therefore it will be true to say now that it is not last year'. However, he will make use of the fact that it is last year in the following case of what is ungenerated but destructible. And he says plausibly that no capacity is for having come to be; for everything past is necessary and cannot be said to be either possible or contingent.[468]

283b14-17 And equally in the case of what formerly was everlasting [but later is not: for this will have the potentiality for something which is not in actuality; so that if we assume the capacity it will be true to say now that this is last year,] and generally at any time past.

Having shown that it follows for someone who maintains that the generable can be indestructible that it will possess the capacity for not existing in respect of the past, he goes on to show that it follows for someone who maintains that the ungenerable can be destructible that it will possess the capacity for existing in respect of the past, which is equally impossible.

For what is ungenerable and everlasting,[469] whenever it is destroyed, will possess the capacity it had when it existed, prior to its destruction, which was the capacity for existing. For the substrate persists, possessing the capacity for both opposites. But it will be capable of destruction neither in the present nor in the future; for it will always remain destroyed. Therefore it will possess the capacity for the future for that which it neither is nor is capable of being in actuality, given that it is destroyed for ever. But since it is supposed to possess the capacity generally, whenever we posit what is possible, it will be possible truly to say now that it is a year ago, or generally in any past time, given that it possesses the capacity for being then.[470]

So if this is impossible, then either it will not possess the capacity it had when it existed, which was shown to belong to those things which are generated or exist by nature, or if it does possess it and preserves that capacity it will do so in respect of the future, and will be capable of coming to be in actuality in future in respect of it, and nothing absurd will follow for those who suppose that what is going to exist already exists as there does for those who suppose that the past exists. For someone who posits that what will be exists already posits that thing of which it possesses the capacity, so that it is capable of being in every part of future time; and for this reason it is now supposed to exist.[471]

283b17-22 If then we treat the matter in physical terms, and not in complete generality, [it will be impossible both for something that has previously been everlasting later to become destructible, and for something that previously was not later to be everlasting. For the perishables and the generables are all subject to alteration. Things are changed by way of contraries; and the things which are by nature are destroyed by the same things out of which they are composed].

He said earlier[472] that to anyone inquiring in general about everything, whether something can be generated but indestructible or ungenerated but destructible, it will be clear [whether this is true] in the case of the heaven too; and having up to this point made his demonstrations in general terms he now proposes to prove the same things in physical terms, and on the basis of natural principles.

He takes confirmation from particular cases, so that in this regard too what is now being said differs from the general demonstrations, not only because they are derived from physical rather than general principles (as the foregoing arguments were), but also because [they are derived] from consideration of individual cases in the physical realm. He shows, then, that what is destructible is invariably generated (it being impossible for something destructible to be ungenerated and to be in that sense eternal), and that what has been generated is invariably destroyed (it being impossible for something generated and formerly non-existent to continue to be undestroyed and everlasting for the rest [of time]).

He shows this by first assuming the following axioms. First, that what is generable and destructible is certainly also alterable (he will demonstrate this is in *On Generation and Corruption*):[473] for generations and destructions occur when things alter and change in respect of quality. He made use of this at the beginning of the book[474] when he showed that the divine body is unalterable, given that it is ungenerated and indestructible.

Secondly, he assumes that what alters and changes in respect of quality, since qualities are distinguished in respect of contrarieties, is altered by its contraries. And third, [he assumes] that what is generated is generated out of contraries and what is destroyed is destroyed into contraries, as is shown in the *Physics*.[475] He employed this at the beginning of the book[476] when he showed that the heaven is ungenerated and indestructible from the fact that it has no contrary. And having recalled that these things have been rigorously demonstrated, by supplying them in order, he presented the whole demonstration concerning the issues at hand in the following form.

Everything generable and destructible is at all events alterable as well, and what alters does so by means of contraries, and what is altered is so by means of contraries; and since in general what is altered by contraries possesses contraries because it is generable and destructible, it is generated from contraries and destroyed into contraries. Therefore everything that is generated is both generated from its contrary and destroyed into its contrary, and similarly everything that is destroyed. Consequently the generated, since, being alterable, it has a contrary, is at all events both generated from its contrary and is destroyed into its contrary. Therefore it is impossible for what is generated to be indestructible, and in this way everlasting. And so in turn the destructible, since it too is alterable and possesses a contrary, is not only destroyed into its contrary but is also generated from its contrary. Consequently it is impossible for something destructible to be ungenerated and in this way everlasting.

One must note that Aristotle calls the ungenerable everlasting even if it is assumed to be destructible, on the grounds that it has no beginning of its generation even if it has a limit to its existence, and likewise the indestructible, even though it is said to have been generated, is also called everlasting on account of its having an uninterrupted existence for the rest [of time]. He knows the distinction between this, which is everlasting in one direction, and that which is in both, as he makes clear by his clear distinction of that which exists for an infinite time into that [which is infinite] *simpliciter* (which is that in both directions) and which is [infinite] from a certain point (which is that in one direction), when he says 'but that which is for an infinite time, whether *simpliciter* or from a certain point, obtains either always, or for the most part'.[477]

Alexander, after the end of his exegesis of the book, once again recalls the passage where Aristotle says 'to say that there is nothing to prevent something generated from being indestructible',[478] and tries to respond to Plato, who says from a position of greater strength that, while everything which is bodily in form is dissoluble and destructible in its own nature, yet through the goodness of the divine will which directly produces the heaven, the heaven continues to be undissolved and immortal.[479]

He [sc. Alexander] says that what is receptive of something is so either contingently, so that it is capable of receiving the contraries too, or necessarily; and while what possesses the capacity contingently can be prevented by something from changing into the other opposite, those things in which this capacity is rather said to be of necessity are incapable *simpliciter* of coming to be their opposite. For what is impossible *simpliciter* cannot be brought about by anything.

'Of impossibilities', he says,

> some, such as lifting this particular weight, which are impossible for some would be possible for others, while others, whose underlying nature is unreceptive and whose opposites hold of necessity, are impossible *simpliciter*, and impossible for everybody, such as making the diagonal commensurable with the side, or twice two equal five.

Since things are so,

he says,

> let us see how the capacity for being destroyed belongs to the destructibles, whether it is possible for them not to be destroyed, or whether they will necessarily be destroyed. If [it does so] contingently, it would be possible for something which is of its own nature destructible not to be destroyed, since this kind of contingent is what is capable both of being generated and of not being generated. But since none of the things which are of their own nature destructible are capable of not being destroyed, the necessity for destruction must hold of necessity for the destructibles. And if this is necessary, they will be unreceptive of the opposite, namely of not being destroyed. Therefore it is impossible, and impossible for everything, and impossible *simpliciter*, that the destructible not be destroyed. And as this is the case,

he says,

> do the people who say these things say that everything is possible for God, or do they say that some things are impossible even for him? For if there were some things that were according to these people impossible for God, it is clear that they would be so in their own nature. But they do hold that some things are impossible even for God; for in saying 'but evils cannot be destroyed, Theodorus, ...[480] nor can these things take their place among the gods, but they must frequent mortal nature and this place of necessity',[481] he says that there is something such as to be impossible even for God. For if,

he says,

> it were possible for him, what could he have preferred instead of it? But if things which are in their nature impossible are also impossible for the gods, and it is impossible in its nature for something destructible not to be destroyed, and the world is destructible, it will be impossible even for God that the world be not at some time destroyed.[482] For if this impossibility were possible for him, why should he not have made each of the other generable and destructible things indestructible? For in each case it is reasonable to suppose that the divine is without envy.[483]

Since Alexander wrote these things in these very words, someone might wonder why he did not bring up the same things against Aristotle's demonstration in the eighth book of the *Physics*[484] that the heaven is limited in size in its own nature, and that a limited body has limited power, and that it is in eternal motion because of the power directly instilled in it by the immobile cause which is always similarly disposed towards the same things. For how does saying this differ from saying that while it [sc. the heaven] is not wholly immortal on the grounds that it is generated, still it will neither be dissolved nor chance upon the fate of death, on the grounds that it enjoys directly and without mediation the divine goodness? For it would be possible to question Aristotle's argument too.[485]

How, then, can limitation of power belong to the heaven? Is it in such a way as also to admit of its not actually being limited, or is it limited of necessity? And if contingently, one might infer that some other limited body might also possess infinite power; but if of necessity, one could say that it is therefore impossible for everybody and impossible *simpliciter*, so that it will be impossible even for God to make a limited power unlimited.

But while the similarity of the arguments is self-evident, I think, even to those who do not see very clearly, Alexander did not realise that both Plato and Aristotle, in saying that the heaven is generated and is directly moved by God,[486] know that eternal existence and motion were given to the heaven by God neither contingently nor unnaturally, but necessarily and naturally. And as they wished to point out, for reasons of piety, that these things are God-given, and did not spring from corporeal nature, having separated the generated from the producer and the moved from the mover conceptually, they showed that while corporeal nature is no more capable of eternal existence and eternal motion than it is of self-subsistence, God is responsible for these things.

When Plato wished to show in the *Statesman*[487] how the whole arrangement and cosmic ordering was supplied to the corporeal element by the Demiurge, he separated the Demiurge conceptually [from the rest] and showed the world degenerating into disorder. In the same way in this context they wanted to show that the nature of the corporeal element in itself is simple, possibly, or [that it is derived] from the perfection of the four elements, spherical, limited, and revolving. And [they wanted to show] that the direct activity of the Demiurge was to cause eternal existence and eternal motion, and that God is not only responsible for what is corporeal in form itself, its figure,[488] and for the other things which are joined essentially with it, but that as soon as these things, which are considered in themselves [divine],[489] have come to be, greater and more divine goods belong to them as a result of God's excellence which gives itself to them.[490]

And the argument says nothing other than that what belongs to the world insofar as it is generated and limited, as if it were self-subsistent,[491] and what else [belongs to it] insofar as it is directly dependent upon God, and for this reason suitable for more complete participation from him. For just as it is generable and limited in itself, so too it is suitable for eternal existence and eternal motion.[492]

So it is not true to say *simpliciter* that the world is destructible in its own nature. For its whole nature is to be considered along with its suitability in relation to the Demiurge, through which it has itself a share of the eternal goods. But the argument seeks to separate inseparables[493] in order to consider both the corporeal element of the world and the goodness of God in themselves.[494]

And it is, I think, unworthy of Alexander's seriousness to say that if it were possible for God to destroy evil he would have wished for nothing rather than that, and to say 'why then has he not made each of the other generable and destructible things indestructible? For in each case it is reasonable to suppose that the divine is without envy'.[495] For in the first place, these are the words of a man who considers God's power to be weaker than his will. And what impediment could there be to the will of God who has produced the natures of every being? If he had thought it to be good that there be no evil at all, why has he made room for it [sc. evil] to insinuate itself into beings, by making the lowest of them of such a kind such that evil could arise along with them? And I say these things against Alexander who does not want to say that there are two principles of beings,[496] but is persuaded to posit only one principle by Aristotle's insistence that 'a plurality of rulers is not good'.[497]

In the second place, he seems completely unaware of the import of what is said in *Theaetetus* concerning evil, as a result of which he omits the most important part of the doctrine in his exposition of the passage, namely 'for it is necessary that there be something opposed to the good'.[498] For the text reads as follows: 'but evils cannot be destroyed, Theodorus, for it is necessary that there be something opposed to the good', etc.

For if God had existed as far as the heaven in the progression of his activity, evil would have had no entrance into beings. But since God exists as the fount of all goodness, he did not pass over that lowest goodness in the sublunary realm, where there is generation and destruction, and where not only the form but also the privation of the form are necessarily produced,[499] so that something contrarily opposed to the lowest good is generated, which is considered as its privation. If this were not the case, then the lowest thing opposite to it would not be good, nor would God be the cause of all goodness. Consequently God will not wish evils to perish, since he would thus also wish the goods opposed to them to perish and he himself no longer to be the cause of all goodness.[500]

But if someone were to say 'what is there to prevent these goods from being while evils do not exist?', he would not realise that these goods would no longer exist. For there would not be human justice and temperance if it were not possible for them to be worn down and transformed into their privations, nor would there be health among the animals consisting of the elements[501] if they could not also grow sick. There would still be the powers of the souls and the infinitudes of the divine bodies; but this genus of souls and bodies[502] would be completely excised from the world, and the world would not yet be complete, since it would not be filled with the lowest goods; and the first lowest goods and those completed without toil and perfectly distant from matter would seem in no way to be differentiated.

See what a great and multiple cause of evils would be the loss of evils! And it is clear that if he [sc. God] were to wish it [sc. evil] not to exist, he would not be good. But Plato rightly both understood and conveyed to later generations that evil must necessarily exist and arise adventitiously for the sake of the good. From what he says it is perfectly clear that it would not have been good to make all of the generated and destructible things and the lowest things of the world indestructible. And [it is also clear] that what is of its own nature destructible, such as man, if it were made indestructible, would in fact be completely destroyed. For what is indestructible is no longer a man,[503] but something greater and of some other nature, of which there are many in the world before [one gets to] the lowest things.

Having condemned the admirable Alexander in the case of this matter for the sake of those who are sometimes led astray by the man's views, I shall put hereabouts an end to my exposition of the first book *On the Heavens*, praying that I may appear to be worthy of those who give praise, and of heaven, and of God's magnificence in heaven.[504]

Notes

1. Or: 'having made these things clear'; this refers to the argument of the previous two chapters for the necessary uniqueness of the world (*Cael.* 1.8-9; Simplicius, *in Cael.* 1.8-9, 247,28-292,7; Hankinson, 2003).
2. Reading *hikanôs*, with Ec, against *kalôs* of Heiberg and the other MSS of Simplicius: when the passage is quoted below (293,7) all the MSS read *hikanôs*. The MSS of Aristotle here all read *hikanôs*, except for J which reads *hikanon*; and Simplicius quotes the sentence with *hikanôs*: 293,7. The sense (as distinct from the tone) is not in any case affected.
3. In general, I translate *genêtos* and *agenêtos* as 'generated' and 'ungenerated', while rendering *phthartos* and *aphthartos* as 'destructible' and 'indestructible'. In Greek, each of these adjectives may carry either a modal or an absolute force, and in some cases 'generable' is to be preferred for *genêtos*, as conversely on occasion 'destroyed' is for *phthartos*. Aristotle himself is well aware of the ambiguity in the terms, and devotes *Cael.* 1.11 to an analysis of their multiplicity of meanings. The justification for my preference is that Aristotle (and hence Simplicius) is in general talking about *this* world, and hence of whether or not as a matter of fact it has been generated (if it has then it immediately follows that it is, or at least was, generable); on the other hand, it is a moot point whether or not it is even susceptible of destruction (although Aristotle thinks that if it *is* so susceptible, then it will as a matter of fact be destroyed: *Cael.* 1.12). David Sedley has suggested rendering these terms as 'subject to generation', 'subject to destruction', etc., which does succeed in capturing (more or less) the ambiguity, but at the expense of a certain awkwardness.
4. See n. 1 above.
5. See 293,11-295,29.
6. This is the standard interpretation of the view presented by Plato in the *Timaeus* (esp. 41A-B): but see below, 294,7-10; nn. 24-5.
7. The position Aristotle himself will defend: below, 1.12; he also apparently believes it to be uniquely his (below, 279b12-13), a position endorsed by Simplicius (293,11-13). But depending upon how precisely one is to characterise the identity-conditions for a cosmos (see below, nn. 8, 131-3, 135), this view may be ascribed to Xenophanes, Heraclitus (but see 279b14-17 below), and (in a sense) Parmenides and the Eleatics; and on one view it was also the position of Plato (see below, 294,7-10; nn. 24-5).
8. The atomists, Leucippus and Democritus (and later Epicurus), all held that this cosmos was only one of infinitely many that have occurred and will continue to do so, each of them merely temporarily stable agglomerations of atoms (Leucippus: 67 A 1 DK = Diogenes Laertius 9.31; cf. 67 A 24 DK; Democritus: 68 B 167 DK = Simplicius, *in Phys.* 327,23-6; 68 A 40 DK = Hippolytus 1.13.2; Epicurus, *ad Hdt.* 45, cf. 74-5; *ad Pyth.* 88; Lucretius 2.1052-

1104). Anaximander too apparently held that there were distinct worlds at least serially, and perhaps also concurrently (12 A 9-10 DK), but this is controversial (cf. KRS, 122-6). In their different ways Empedocles (31 B 17 = Simplicius, *in Phys.* 158,1-35; cf. 31 B 27-31 DK; and see 293,20-294,3 below) and the Stoics (Plutarch, *On Stoic Self-Contradictions* 1052c-1053b = *SVF* 2.604-5 = 46D-E LS; cf. *SVF* 1.98, 1.1052, 2.589, 2.596) thought that the cosmos was at various times reduced to complete homogeneity, out of which, in turn, differentiation arose, which might be interpreted as the successive generation and destruction of distinct *kosmoi* (depending on what are supposed to be the appropriate conditions for cosmos-identity: see 307,20-308,22, and nn. 131-3, 135 below), although Aristotle apparently ranges Empedocles (and Heraclitus) among the single-world theorists (279b14-17; 293,15-20; 294,31-3 below). In Simplicius' time, the hypothesis of the world's being generated and destructible was also of course the view of Christians such as Philoponus, much to Simplicius' distaste (see C. Wildberg, *Philoponus: Against Aristotle on the Eternity of the World* [London, 1987]); see nn. 38, 46, 97, 130 below.

9. Aristotle's treatises often do begin with a detailed and critical examination of the views of his predecessors (cf. e.g. *DA* 1; *Phys.* 1.1-4; *Metaph.* 1); as he writes at the beginning of *Metaph.* 2 (2.1, 993a30-b1): 'the study of reality is in a way difficult, in a way easy; an indication of this is that while no one can reasonably get a grip on all of it, we cannot all fail either': everybody is right about something, no one about everything. Elsewhere, Aristotle often remarks that the starting-points for philosophical inquiry are reputable opinions (*endoxa*), which he characterises as being the views of either the many or the wise (*Top.* 1.1, 100b21-3; cf. *EN* 1.4, 1095a18-19): the *Topics* is devoted, as he says at the outset (1.1, 100a18-24), to analysing arguments involving such views. The best example of the appeal to *endoxa* as part of philosophical methodology occurs in the discussion of weakness of the will in *EN* 7.1-3, where various opinions on the matter are laid out and tested for consistency.

10. In spite of this remark, Simplicius appears in what follows to enumerate only two advantages possessed by the procedure.

11. See n. 8 above; *Metaph.* 3 is a compilation of difficulties, *aporiai*, which beset the practice of metaphysics, and as such serves as a preliminary to the proper investigation as such.

12. i.e. the opposing views and the considerations urged in their favour.

13. It is not clear whether Simplicius intends to contrast the presentations of the historical figures concerned with those of their namesakes in Platonic dialogue, or rather he means that, within the contexts of the dialogues, the views of the sophists are better presented by Socrates in order to rebut them than they are in the mouths of their protagonists. In view of the generality of the claim ('no Callicles, etc.'), the former cannot be ruled out, even if it is hard to imagine Thrasymachus himself being less sympathetic in person than the caricature portrayed by Plato in *Republic* 1; but on balance the latter is the likelier option. Callicles is the interlocutor of the *Gorgias*, and a mouthpiece for the latter's views on rhetoric; Protagoras appears as a character in the dialogue of the same name, and his views are extensively discussed in the first half of the *Theaetetus*.

14. *katadikazesthai*.

15. *katapsêphizesthai*.

16. *katadikazein*.

17. This is controversial: see n. 7 above.

18. On the Orphic material, which is multifarious, contradictory, and deriving from a wide variety of sources and epochs, see KRS, ch. 1, §4; for Hesiod, see

Theogony 116-34; 726-45; and see KRS, ch. 1, §5; both sources clearly describe a variety of cosmic origins: but I have not been able to find any confirmation of Simplicius' claim that they both maintain the subsequent eternity of the created world.

19. The phraseology strongly suggests that Simplicius has the atomists exclusively in mind here: the successive worlds are numerically quite distinct, and contain different material parts, and not merely reconstitutions of previous ones. The atomists held that even if an individual qualitatively indistinguishable from Socrates were to recur (as will happen in their temporally infinite universe), it will not be Socrates. Indeed, even if all of Socrates' original component atoms were so re-constituted, the result would still not be Socrates *redivivus*, at any rate according to Lucretius: 3.830-51.

20. A line is missing here (and in the almost identical quotations at *in Phys.* 158,7-13 and *in Cael.* 1.3, 141,1-6); it can be supplied from l.8 of the parallel Fr. 31 B 26.5-12 DK (*in Phys.* 33,23-30): 'Thus insofar as they have learned to become one out of many.'

21. Fr. 31 B 17.7-13 DK; cf. 31 B 26.5-12 DK.

22. 22 B 30 DK. The complete fragment reads: 'this world, which is the same for everything, no god or man made, but it has been always, is, and shall be an everliving fire, kindled in measures and extinguished in measures'; see further below, 294,15-16.

23. See n. 8 above.

24. For this dispute over interpretation, see further 299,22-30 below; the 'theologians' presumably here at least include the Neoplatonists (see n. 25 below), although elsewhere (293,13; 296,5) the reference is less clear (see n. 39 below).

25. i.e. there is no particular generation in time, according to these theorists; the 'generation' involved is the continuous dependency of the lower elements in the cosmos on the sustaining power of the higher ones (as their 'productive cause': 299,22-30 below), a Neoplatonist commonplace: cf. Proclus, *Elements of Theology*, 1-57, esp. 1-7, 18-20; and see Simplicius, *in Cael.* 1.3, 92,33-96,12 (Hankinson, 2002a).

26. i.e. known to the intellect.

27. *in Cael.* 1.3, 140,25-141,9, where he also discusses this fragment.

28. In the earlier passage (*in Cael.* 1.3, 140,25-141,9), Simplicius holds that Empedocles is referring 'in an enigmatic manner, as is the custom of the Pythagoreans' to the unified, intelligible, unchanging world of pure Being when he speaks of the cosmos unified by Love, and to the ordinary, changeable, perceptible world of Becoming when talking about the world distinguished by Strife, and holds that these distinct states are concurrent, and that the talk of one coming to be from the other and *vice versa* is merely metaphorical 'as Aristotle was well aware' (141,9-10); here Simplicius again betrays his syncretising, Neoplatonist sensibilities, this proto-Platonising Empedocles being a wholly fantastical creation.

29. See above, n. 22.

30. i.e. into the pure, undifferentiated fire that punctuates each cosmic cycle: 22 B 30-1 DK = Clement, *Miscellanies* 5.14.104.1-5; 90 DK = Plutarch, *On the 'E' at Delphi* 388d-e; cf. Diogenes Laertius 9.7-8.

31. See Frs 67 A 1 DK; 68 A 40 DK; and see n. 8 above.

32. i.e., even if a precisely congruent arrangement of the same material parts is recreated, the resulting 'recreation' will be numerically distinct from its predecessor (see nn. 7-8 above, 131-3, 135 below), presumably simply on the grounds of its discontinuity with it. Cf. the Epicurean argument for the finality of death: above, n. 19.

33. Empedocles: 31 B 8-12 DK (although these fragments refer to the generation of ordinary things within worlds, and not to the worlds themselves: see n. 36 below); Heraclitus: 22 B 30-1, 90 DK (in the latter case at least, Plutarch sees a reference to the cosmic cycle of world generation from and resolution into fire: see n. 30 above).

34. The word is the peculiar *den* (cf. 68 B 156 DK = Plutarch, *Against Colotes* 4, 1108f.), often taken to be a Democritean coinage formed by dropping the negative prefix *ou* ('not') from *ouden* ('nothing'), and hence sometimes rendered 'hing'; but I follow Barnes (1979 2, 100-1, and n. 11) in supposing that it is a genuine, albeit rare, word (it is attested in a fragment of Alcaeus: 130 LP), and hence choose the non-exotic translation 'thing'.

35. Aristotle, Fr. 208 R, from Aristotle's *On Democritus*.

36. Some such supplement seems necessary here: perhaps read *kai gar kaiper* for *kai gar kai*: 'and in fact although ...', although this is difficult in view of the indicative verb *phêsin* in the next line (LSJ s.v. *kaiper* note that the cases of *kaiper* + indicative are dubious), although that too could be emended (to *phêi*). The run of the argument is even so a little obscure. First, Simplicius is here talking of Empedocles' generation of successive phases of the cosmic cycle out of Love and Strife (above, 293,25-294,3), and not of ordinary 'generation' and 'destruction' (which are the subject-matter of Frs 31 B 8-12 DK: above, n. 33); and the point appears to be that even though Empedocles is not committed to successive phases of the unified Love-stage (or the discriminated Strife-stage) being the same in anything other than general type (and hence that, for all he says explicitly, it might involve genuine generation and destruction), nevertheless he does not so conceptualise it, but rather sees it as (at bottom) a case of alteration. And while there is no extant fragment that definitely tells in favour of this view, it is indeed a natural one to ascribe to him, in view of his evident desire to evade the Parmenidean strictures on generation *ex nihilo* by insisting that, at some level, all generation really is re-arrangement.

37. 'Even Alexander', since he explicitly denied that Heraclitus' cycle involved mere alteration: above, 294,16-30.

38. The reference here is presumably to Christians, such as Simplicius' contemporary and arch-enemy Philoponus; see nn. 8 above, 46, 97, 130 below.

39. Here the reference can hardly be to the Neoplatonists (see n. 24 above), at least if Simplicius implies that Alexander ascribed this view to them (the text is compatible with his only attributing the view to Plato – but that is a less likely reading); perhaps he means to include Platonists of all casts (including, e.g., Galen, who accepted the demiurgic construction of the world).

40. Simplicius is arguing that when Aristotle affirms the ungenerability of the world he is not in fact in opposition to the view of Plato in the *Timaeus* properly understood, where (in Simplicius' opinion) the generation of the world in time is not at issue (see below, 296,16-22); and so once more Aristotle is not actually disagreeing with Plato, only with a natural but mistaken understanding (namely that the world was generated in time) of what he said (this is the point of the first sentence of the paragraph); see n. 86 below.

41. i.e., rather than being in a condition of full actuality, it is in one of continuous process, which is the standard Platonic way of characterising the visible world: *Tim.* 27D-28A, 49B-52B; *Theaet.* 152D-E, 157A-58A; cf. *Rep.* 5, 476B-80A.

42. Fr. 206 Rose; whatever the rights and wrongs of Simplicius' standard

Neoplatonist atemporal interpretation of the generation story of the *Timaeus*, it is clearly fantastical to suppose that Aristotle subscribed to it; and this fragment has absolutely no tendency to show that he did.

43. *Tim.* 38B.

44. The argument is apparently that, no matter how large a stretch of time you take as being that of some current existence, there will always be a time before it and a time after it – and so time is unbounded in both directions. But it is hard to see why there should be a time before any stretch of time, given Plato's claim that time came to be along with the universe. In other words, there was no time before the existence of the universe – but that does not entail that there has been an infinity of past time. Simplicius supposes that to 'come to be at a particular time' entails that that moment of time is defined by its position within the temporal sequence, i.e. by the stretches of time before it and after it – but that is simply to beg the question at issue; see below, n. 65.

45. Or perhaps: 'set out Plato's views in a suspect manner'; this latter seems better to fit the Greek, but the translation I have preferred makes better sense and is I think possible.

46. Probably a reference to his Christian opponents, in particular Philoponus, against whose *Against Aristotle on the Eternity of the World* he has spent so much time arguing in the earlier parts of *in Cael.*: see Wildberg, 1987; and nn. 8, 38, 97, 130.

47. For this stock Platonic phrase, see *Tim.* 27D-28A; and see 297,27; 298,9-24; 300,6-28; 301,9; 305,15 below; *in Cael.* 1.12, 352,33; n. 447.

48. i.e. it is in a constant, continuous, eternal process of generation and destruction, which never comes to completion; but it has not itself ever actually come to be in a temporal sense.

49. *Tim.* 27D; cf. *in Cael.* 1.3, 104,5-6; and see below, 299,7-8.

50. *Tim.* 27C.

51. Plato's text here reads 'whether it always was'; and Simplicius himself later quotes the same passage with 'always': see below, 298,26.

52. *Tim.* 28B.

53. i.e. it is not *actually* coming to be as a whole, although it may involve constant processes of generation; cf. n. 48 above.

54. Perhaps, reading *legoi* in place of *legoien*, 'if he were to say ...'.

55. *tôi gar houtôs apthartôi to houtôs genêton antikeitai*: it may be preferable to read *pthartôi* in place of *apthartôi*, and take *antikeitai* in its sense of 'is the opposite of' (the sense it clearly bears, e.g., at 300,20-2), yielding the translation: 'since "generated" in this sense is the opposite of "destroyed" in this sense'.

56. The Greek here is extremely odd, and the text may well be corrupt; it is perhaps better to seclude *homologountos* ('given that he agrees with this') here; or perhaps to emend to *homologoumenou*, yielding 'to say that it has come to be from an agreed beginning'.

57. This is a cardinal principle of Aristotle's, and the principal subject of *Cael.* 1.12; and while there is no explicit evidence of Plato's accepting it, as Alexander here assumes (as Simplicius points out: 300,16-20), he does accept the corollary that everything generated is destructible: see n. 75 below.

58. Since 'is' (*esti*), in such cases, is reserved for that which properly and unqualifiedly is, and as such is contrasted with that which is merely becoming: see the texts cited in n. 41 above.

59. i.e. it must 'have come to be' in a genuine temporal sense: cf. n. 47 above.

60. *Tim.* 28B-C.

61. cf. *Cael.* 1.4, 271a17-28; see *in Cael.* 1.4, 149,1-154,5; *Phys.* 8.9, 265a27-b1.

62. *Tim.* 27D; see 297,15-16 above.

63. i.e. Alexander, in his desire to portray Plato as arguing only for a temporal origin, overlooks the passage just quoted where he explicitly distinguishes between things (such as the visible world) which are always in process, and those (the intelligibles) which always are in full actuality.

64. *Tim.* 28B; 297,20-1 above.

65. Simplicius appears to hold that anything which comes to be must do so at a particular moment, or 'now' as he calls it, and any 'now' is the boundary between a stretch of both past and future time. Aristotle does in fact treat 'nows' as demarcating stretches of past and future time (*Phys.* 4.12, 220b5-10; cf. 4.11, 219b9-220a26); but there seems no good reason for denying the possibility that there can be a first instant of time coinciding with the beginning of the generation of the cosmos; see above, n. 44.

66. *Tim.* 38B.

67. *Tim.* 28A.

68. *Tim.* 28C.

69. *Tim.* 28B.

70. *ontôs on*, a favourite Platonic formula: see *Tim.* 28A (quoted below, 300,8-9); see also 301,16; and cf. e.g. *Phdr.* 247E.

71. i.e. its being corporeal in nature would not amount to a reason why it came to be *in time*, although it clearly would supply a reason for its being 'generated' in the sense of its being dependent on higher-order, non-physical realities. Here again Simplicius' Neoplatonism shows itself.

72. i.e. non-self-movers ('move' here to be taken in a broad sense to cover all sorts of change and affection) owe their existence to something independent of themselves, and hence are in a constant state of being produced; again the language here is characteristically Neoplatonic.

73. cf. 297,28-298,1 above; this is a very close repetition of that sentence from Alexander (there are only a couple of minor linguistic divergences), and it should probably be treated as a re-quotation.

74. *Tim.* 28A: Plato's actual subject here is 'what is believed as a result of opinion and irrational perception'.

75. *Rep.* 8, 546A; cf. n. 57 above. Simplicius' argument is that Plato could not have meant that the world was temporally generated but temporally indestructible, as Alexander has it, because that is incompatible with the principle here enunciated – but on this interpretation, it is hard to see why Plato should have bothered to make an issue of its actual indestructibility, as he does; moreover at *Tim.* 41A-B, the Demiurge, in his speech to the lesser gods, describes the created world as intrinsically destructible (since anything composite can be pulled apart), although it will never, as a result of Demiurgic fiat, actually be destroyed – and again, this is hard to make sense of on the Simplician continuous-process account of becoming.

76. Again, this ignores the modal distinction between its being destructible on the one hand, but never actually being destroyed on the other (above, n. 75), as does 300,27-301,1 below; however, Aristotle at least supposed that what is destructible must at some time be destroyed: see *Cael.*1.12, and 351,15-353,10 below.

77. cf. 298,1-6 above.

78. cf. 298,6-10; Simplicius here is effectively endorsing the Aristotelian position that generability and destructibility are mutually entailing (argued for at length in *Cael.* 1.12; see *in Cael.* 1.12, below), and arguing on the basis of that that Plato cannot have supposed that the world was temporally generated but temporally indestructible; but of course there is no reason to suppose that Plato would have endorsed it too.

79. 298,12-13.

80. *Phys.* 8.10 argues that the cause of an eternal (i.e. infinite) motion cannot itself be limited (266a12-24), while a finite magnitude cannot contain an infinite force (266a24-b6), and this is presumably what Simplicius is referring to here; this is part of Aristotle's proof of the immateriality of the Prime Mover. However, *pace* Simplicius (and others), the Prime Mover plays no role in *Cael.*, all responsibility for the eternal motion of the heavens being assigned to their elemental nature (see especially *Cael.* 1.2-4); that capacity is limited in one sense (the heavens are limited in extent, and move with a determinate speed), but unlimited temporally. And even if Simplicius is right that Aristotle does, on occasion and in a sense, ascribe responsibility for all motion including that of the heavens to divine influence, this does not show that the heavens owe their existence (and hence their eternity as such) to divine influence; they need not be derivative beings in the Neoplatonic sense (see nn. 25, 71-2 above).

81. This is a requotation of 298,16-18, although Heiberg does not mark it as such.

82. *Tim.* 37E; i.e. it is an eternal existent, and ordinary considerations of time and tense do not apply to it.

83. *to paradeigma*, the exemplar of the eternal truths the image of which the Demiurge creates in the visible world.

84. *Tim.* 37D.

85. Simplicius is alluding to Aristotle's own remarks concerning his relations with Plato at *EN* 1.6, 1096a14-17: 'yet surely it would be thought better, and indeed necessary for the preservation of truth, even to destroy one's own views, and most particularly if we are philosophers; for both of these things are dear to us: but it is right to honour the truth the more'.

86. Or perhaps more generally 'of words'; again, Simplicius betrays his Neoplatonist syncretising tendencies: he sees Aristotle not as refuting Plato himself, but refuting a mistaken interpretation of Plato's words: see above, 296,6-11; n. 40.

87. *epagôgê* is not strictly induction (in the modern sense of a pattern of inference) but rather the enumeration of a number of similar cases: cf. *Top.* 1.12, 105a10-19.

88. *Cael.* 1.10, 279b20-1.

89. All of this is standard Aristotelian doctrine (see e.g. *Metaph.* 9.3), as long as 'prior' is interpreted (as it clearly should be here) as 'prior in time'; for Aristotle actualities are metaphysically prior to potentialities (see *Metaph.* 9.8); in fact they are even in a sense prior in time, but only in that something possessing the actuality in question must exist prior to the existence of such a potentiality in something else (*Metaph.* 9.8, 1049b17-27).

90. This argument relies on a version of the 'Principle of Plenitude' (PP), a version of which is to play a key role in *Cael.* 1.12, to the effect that if something genuinely possesses a capacity for something, in an infinite time that capacity must at some time be realised. Hence, given that the world is generated, its component parts evidently possess the capacity for existing in a disorderly state (or at any rate in a differently ordered state), since they once did so – but if they still possess that capacity (and there is no reason why they should not), then at some time in the future they will come to be differently disposed, and hence this world, considered as being this disposition of the elements, cannot last for ever.

91. 279b31.

92. Read *ginomenon* for *genomenon*.

93. *Tim.* 38B; cf. 37D.

94. *Pol.* 272E-73E.

95. i.e. by making some counterfactual supposition; see below, 303,33-307,11.

96. i.e., on Simplicius' view, the references to the 'prior' disorderly conditions of things 'before' the organisational intervention of the Demiurge, have no temporal reference, but simply refer to the thought-experiment of supposing the world not to be so organised: see below, 305,20-307,11.

97. i.e. the Christians (cf. nn. 38, 130) – the sarcasm of his tone suggests that Simplicius has Philoponus principally in mind here.

98. This appeal to the Principle of Sufficient Reason (PSR) in generation goes back at least to Parmenides: Fr. 21 B 8.9 DK; see further n. 138 below; and *in Cael.* 1.12, nn. 414, 418, 426, 434.

99. This sentence of Aristotle's text is missing, either from the end of this lemma or the beginning of the next. It seems to belong rather here.

100. Xenocrates (396-314 BC) was the third head of the Academy, the successor of Speusippus and Plato, and here Simplicius explicitly attributes to him (and unnamed 'Platonists') the doctrine that the world had no beginning in time; since of course he believes this to have been Plato's view as well (and to have been Aristotle's view of Plato), he must mean only that Xenocrates made this interpretation explicit (see Isnardi Parente, 1982, Fr. 100); in fact, of course he is (inadvertently) right in supposing that Aristotle had people other than Plato himself (to whom he attributes temporal generation of the cosmos) in mind here.

101. *Tim.* 30A.

102. In this paragraph Simplicius supposes, as Aristotle apparently does too (*Meteor.* 1.3, 340b5-11 even implies this of the celestial element) that none of the elements ever exists in its pure actuality, and hence that the process of arriving at the concept of an element is one of conceptual rather than physical decomposition of composite objects.

103. i.e., in the case of geometrical constructions an actual first moment of their physical construction – and this helps the geometer to unpack the structure of the figures; cf. 304,6-10 above.

104. i.e. in the cube the planes themselves do not coincide, although the points and lines of their edges and vertices do.

105. The MSS do not contain 'or earth' (*ê gê*) here; but it seems that it should be added.

106. i.e. the triangle contains lines – but it is not necessary to suppose that they existed before the construction of the triangle.

107. Reading *kai kata khronon* with c. If the MSS reading is retained, it would translate as 'it is necessary for generation and time to be real', which is possible, but in view of 305,33 (and the general sense) less likely. It is probable that 305,6 below should also be changed similarly.

108. Or possibly, reading *kai kata khronon, diorizousan* for *kai khronon diorizonta*, 'but rather genuine generation in time, which distinguishes'; cf. n. 107; and 305,33 below.

109. cf. *Tim.* 27D-28A.

110. i.e. although they did not *actually* temporally precede them.

111. i.e. the thing generated: the lines from which the triangle is 'generated' are still there in the actual triangle.

112. Deleting Heiberg's question-mark in favour of a full stop.

113. Fr. 31 B 8.3 DK; see n. 33 above.

114. There seems to be a slip here: one would expect Simplicius to say 'through the destruction of *earth, or fire*, or what is in between', since 'the intermediate' often stands for the intermediate elements, i.e. water and air (cf.

e.g. *Cael.* 1.8, 276b1-2); and while 'intermediate' can have other references (e.g. to air and fire, the rising elements intermediate between the revolving element and the falling elements: 277b13-17), none of them seem appropriate in this context; but there is insufficient justification actually to emend here.

115. The element theory is expounded in *Cael.* 3-4, *Meteor.* 4, and *GC* 2; that the elements themselves are mixtures of the four qualities (hot, cold, wet, dry) is expounded at *GC* 2.1-4; on the traditional account, these qualities are realised in Prime Matter, or what the Stoics (whose terminology Simplicius here follows) called 'matter without qualities'; it has recently been questioned whether Aristotle either needs or invokes Prime Matter – but that debate need not concern us. The sense in which matter and form are prior even to Prime Matter and the qualities is not of course compositional (Prime Matter is a type of matter, and being endowed with qualities is a way of being informed), but rather analytical: the general metaphysical distinction between form and matter lies behind all of these physical analyses (for form and matter, see *Phys.* 2.3, *Metaph.* 7-8, esp. 8.6).

116. cf. *GC* 2.1-3, 7-8.

117. I have not been able to find any instances of Aristotle employing the language of production (as opposed to that of generation, in the sense of serial generation of one element from another: *GC* 2.4-5) in these contexts; but Simplicius' point, that, although in Aristotle's theory there is no time before the elements exist, still it is possible to say that the prior principles are responsible for the elements, is reasonable, albeit misguided in the context.

118. cf. 280a7-8.

119. Simplicius makes use here of Aristotelian categories; matter is by definition that without particular form but with the potential for either possessing or failing to possess that form (e.g. *Metaph.* 5.4, 1014b26-1015a19; 7.3, 1029a20-1; 7.15, 1039b29-31; 8.1, 1042a25-b8); matter is also (and equivalently) what persists through change, where change is conceptualised as a motion (in either direction) between the possession of some form and its privation (*Phys.* 1.6-9, esp. 189a20-b27, 190a13-b23, 191a5-14, 191b13-29, 192a25-34); on privation, see *Metaph.* 5.22.

120. In other words there is no such thing (except conceptually) as matter totally devoid of form of any kind: everything has to be something or other.

121. *Pol.* 272E.

122. The MSS of Plato, reading *hormên hormêtheis* in place of the *hormên hormêi* of Simplicius' MSS (with the exception of a correction in one of them, almost certainly inserted by a scribe familiar with the text of Plato), yield the translation: 'as it turned back and banged together, driven by the opposing impulse of the beginning and the end'; the difference in sense is negligible.

123. *Pol.* 273A.

124. *Pol.* 273B-C.

125. sc. on such a hypothesis (which of course Simplicius rejects as an interpretation of Plato).

126. See references collected in n. 8 above.

127. This parenthesis is curious; if it modifies 'has form', as the word-order suggests, then it looks as though 'completely' (or perhaps 'perfectly') and 'incompletely' ('imperfectly') should be transposed; it is possible (although word-order tells against it) that it modifies 'has been destroyed', in which case it might be allowed to stand; although the best sense would be achieved from the transposition.

128. Which is supposed to be absurd: there must be some sorts of change that the world can undergo without its identity being compromised, otherwise we will not be able to refer to the world as a continuant entity at all (cf. Plato, *Theaet.* 179E-83C on the consequences of radical Heracliteanism).

129. The reference is to Empedocles' homogeneous sphere, the result of the operation of Love on the dispersed elements of the universe as it now is: Frs 31 B 29-31 DK; and see 293,20-3 above, 310,13-15.

130. 'Contemporaries' (*hoi nun*) and 'the new one' (*ho kainos*) are contemptuous references to Christians and the Christian doctrine of the Kingdom of Heaven: see nn. 38, 97.

131. i.e. each world maintains the same structural differentiations in each of its recurrences; Simplicius effectively takes a stand here on the conditions of cosmos-identity (see above, nn. 7-8): identity is a matter of complete congruence of properties (determined by type): thus, for any F, if W_1 exhibits F if and only if W_2 exhibits F, then $W_1 = W_2$; see n. 132 below.

132. This paragraph claims that, since the same causes operate in each cosmic cycle on the same matter, we may expect precisely the same result (an interesting expression of a certain sort of cosmic determinism); the following seems to suggest that even if the arrangements of each cosmic cycle are not precisely congruent with those of every other, then still this will be properly described as the continuity of a single cosmos, the differences being only accidental ones of property and arrangement (cf. 307,25-308,2); but in that case one would expect some sort of connective such as 'moreover', 'but even if' rather than 'consequently' – and perhaps Simplicius' point is simply that the world does not differ in identity (within each cycle) as a result of its exhibiting different properties at different times (cf. n. 131 above).

133. As the following paragraphs make clear, the supposition of destruction and non-recurrence may take one of two distinct forms: (1) that a single world (encompassing all the matter there is) be destroyed, never to recur (it is this which is supposed to be impossible: 280a23-6); (2) that, in an infinite reservoir of matter, worlds may be created and destroyed *seriatim*, but without the recurrence of any particular individual world (280a23; and cf. *Cael.* 1.12). A third possibility, that temporal discontinuities between orderings within a finite material universe may suffice to render each successive ordering a new entity (and as such to encompass the genuine destruction of every previous ordering) is exactly what has been ruled out by the conditions on identity expressed in the previous passage (307,20-308,22: nn. 131-2; see also nn. 8, 32).

134. Here Simplicius expands on the impossibility of option (1) (n. 133 above).

135. This phrase, clumsy in English, expresses the material status of the disordered universe (and connects it in standard Aristotelian fashion with potentiality: above, n. 119): Aristotle sometimes characterises the material relation as 'that out of which' (*to ex hou*; e.g. *Phys.* 2.3, 194b23-6), which became a standard designation in later Greek philosophy for the material cause. See 309,14 below.

136. The Principle of Plenitude again: see n. 90 above. Here the thought seems to be not just that any new cosmic arrangement of the basic material will count as a recurrence of the same world, but rather only one with a precise community of properties; but even on this stricter conception of the material conditions for continuant identity, PP will ensure that numerically the same cosmos will recur (at least if we tolerate temporally discontinuous identity: see nn. 131-2 above).

137. This expresses the converse to PP: nn. 90, 133 above. The argument is that, if there were only one generation from the background material, then there would have been an infinity of past time in which the pre-existing, unformed matter had existed as such – but then it would have been, by the converse of PP, incapable of forming a world (since PP states that if a is capable of being F, then after some determinate period of time it will be F).

138. 'From the non-existent' renders the Greek phrase *ek tou mê ontos*; I have preferred this, here and generally, to the slightly more general, albeit less felicitously English, 'from not being'. The prohibition on generation *ex nihilo* was a Greek commonplace; its supposed *a priori* impossibility drives Parmenides' argument for an unchanging reality (29 B 8.5-21 DK; for the early history of the principle, see A. Mourelatos, 'Pre-Socratic origins of the principle that there are no origins of nothing', *Journal of Philosophy* 78 [1981], 649-65). The whole purpose of Aristotle's analysis of change in *Phys.* 1.1-9 is to show how we can make sense of something's coming to be F from not having been F previously (or indeed coming to be *tout court*) without supposing that either it or its properties literally emerge from nothing.

139. sc. if generation *ex nihilo* were conceivable.

140. See nn. 98, 138 above.

141. See n. 97 above.

142. 280a26-7.

143. See n. 8 above.

144. These lines are so close to Aristotle's at *Cael.* 1.10, 280a12-14 as to merit their being treated as a quotation.

145. Not the forms of each successive world caused by Strife, but rather the forms of the Love-world (the sphere) and the Strife-world (the world); thus for Empedocles each world does not change directly into its successor, but rather does so through the intermediary of the sphere-stage – and hence this process does not correspond to that described by Alexander above. For all that, Aristotle (and Simplicius) still view it as properly speaking a case of alteration (see 310,20-3 below); and the same might be said for the conservation of the entire stock of material in the Democritean world, notwithstanding the fact that *individual* worlds are created and destroyed in it.

146. See nn. 129, 145 above.

147. This sentence is not marked as a question in the text; but the opening 'but perhaps', and the succeeding sentence, both indicate that it is a suggestion which is canvassed only in order to be rebutted.

148. i.e. Empedocles and his followers: although his world goes through two distinct phases, only one of which he wants to call a 'world', none the less the model meets Aristotle's criteria for the continuous existence of a universe, so that any change within it only amounts to alteration. *hôs ep' ekeinôn*, here translated 'as it was for those people', might mean 'as it was in those cases', referring to the generation of worlds similar in form; but in view of the very similar 'according to those' of the next line this is unlikely.

149. i.e. Love and Strife; the quotation (not marked as such by Heiberg) is from *Cael.* 1.10, 280a18-19.

150. sc. but not an infinite number; the question is: why should the fact that the worlds (and their successors) are infinite in number mean that the transition from one to another is a genuine case of generation, but that in the case of finitely many should only count as alteration? It seems intuitively as though the single-world case differs from the many-world case, in that in the latter but not in the former the successor-worlds will differ in material constitution – but again it is a further question how crucial that is to ensuring a change of identity (see nn. 131-3 again). The thought may also be that in a finite system of worlds the same arrangement of the same material will recur in an infinite time, but this is not the case for an infinite supply of material and an infinite number of worlds: but this conflicts with 311,15-19 below: n. 158.

151. Simplicius seems here to envisage Aristotle thinking that it is less unacceptable to suppose that some worlds will be completely annihilated (presumably materially) if there is an infinite stock of material for new worlds to grow out of – but such an assumption is radically at odds with the atomists' actual practice. Aristotle is surely not envisaging annihilation; rather the issue is that canvassed above (nn. 131-3, 135, 140), namely that a recurrent single world must be exactly the same as its predecessors because of its material continuity, whereas in a system of multiple or infinite worlds, the matter of each successive world will be different.

152. 280a27-8.

153. *Cael.* 1.8-9; cf. *Phys.* 3.4-8.

154. This has not in fact already been proved; the text is suspect here, and this should probably be deleted.

155. *Cael.* 2.1.

156. Or: concerning them, sc. the atoms.

157. 280a28-30.

158. i.e. in an infinity of time exactly the same constitutions of exactly the same atomic constituents will recur – and they will be the same worlds as they were before (but see n. 150 above).

159. 280a30-2: i.e., Aristotle does not attribute to Plato the converse, namely that something might never have been generated yet be destroyed.

160. i.e. to both the propositions, that the ungenerated might be destroyed as well as that the generated might be indestructible.

161. This ingenious suggestion of course demands the temporal generation interpretation of the *Timaeus* which Simplicius rejects: prior to the Demiurge's organisation there was for an infinite period of time disorder, which, since the Demiurge decrees that his created order will never fail, has, by that creation, been irrevocably destroyed.

162. *Tim.* 30A.

163. The pleonasm here ('it is clear that ... clearly') is Simplicius' own.

164. This is to be one of the main *probanda* of *Cael.* 1.12.

165. 303,18-19 above; see n. 93.

166. *Phys.* 8.10, esp. 266b25-7.

167. See *Cael.* 1.4; *in Cael.* 1.4, 145,10-156,24, 201,11-205,30 (Hankinson, 2002a).

168. This echoes Aristotle's classification of the argument at 280a32; Aristotle is accustomed to distinguish between arguing *phusikôs*, i.e. on the basis of particular facts about the natures of things, and *logikôs*, on general conceptual grounds: cf. *Cael.* 1.7, 274a19, 275b12; *Phys.* 3.2, 202a21, 5, 204b4-10; *GC* 1.2, 316a10-14.

169. cf. *Phys.* 5.1-2.

170. This sentence has the force of an objection to the line of argument here, and might be placed in inverted commas.

171. i.e. they are multiply ambiguous; this is a standard Aristotelian phrase.

172. i.e. the argument commits no fallacy of equivocation. In *Topics* 1.1, 100b25-101a4, Aristotle distinguishes between argument-types: demonstrative (*apodeiktikoi*), which proceed from necessary true axioms to necessary true theorems by properly valid means; dialectical (*dialektikoi*), where the consequences of generally-accepted principles are validly deduced; and contentious (*eristikoi*), which proceed from principles that appear to be generally accepted, but are not, or are invalidly derived from genuine or apparently general principles; this latter class includes arguments which may be used for instruction (*gumnastikoi*, *peirastikoi*), where arguments are fallaciously constructed for educational purposes (the *Topics* itself is designed for this purpose: 1.2, 101a27-31; cf. 1.11, 105a9); as well as those which are outright sophistical (*sophistikoi*), in which fallacious arguments are propounded with intent to deceive (cf. *Sophistical Refutations*).

173. *khôris ... kinêseôs tinos kai parastasis*, perhaps better 'without change or duration'; but I have preferred the translation in the text for reasons of consistency. The idea is that the result of an instantaneous change, since it involves no extended process of generation, is in a sense ungenerated (although of course this is not the central sense of the term).

174. The point is that there is no process of coming to be in motion; something simply starts moving. If for every process there was a process involved in the process itself starting, then there would indeed be an infinite regress of processes: see *Phys*. 5.2, 225b10-226a23. What is said here does not necessarily rule out the possibility of treating acceleration as a change of a change, although Aristotle never develops the conceptual machinery to deal adequately with acceleration – and neither for that matter does anyone else among the ancients.

175. Here Simplicius launches another trial balloon, against the Aristotelian contentions of *Phys*. 5.2.

176. i.e. of a second-order generation for generation itself.

177. i.e. if there is a change between the state of rest and the state of motion, then there will be a change between the state of rest and that change, and also between that change and the state of motion – and so on.

178. This and subsequent supplements are justified by 314,3-4 above; Simplicius' language is compressed here, but there is no call to emend the text.

179. sc. the changes themselves; the kind of change envisaged is not itself a change in time.

180. Read *kathaper enioi ... legontes legôn*: 280b7-8

181. Reading *phasin* for *phêsi* (Moerbeke's translation has 'aiunt'); this makes this sentence too a citation by Simplicius of Aristotle (280b8-9).

182. sc. touching and moving: 280b9.

183. Simplicius seems to mean that Aristotle intends by the use of the aorist ('have come to be') precisely to indicate that there is no process of coming to be for the thing: at one moment it is not, and the next it has come to be. If this is right, Aristotle is anticipating the position of his later contemporary, Diodorus Cronus, who argued that nothing can actually be moving, although it can *have* moved (Sextus, *Against the Professors* 10.85; cf. *Outlines of Pyrrhonism* 2.244-5): movement takes place by means of instantaneous jerks across a quantised space. But it seems more likely that Aristotle is simply making a tense-logical point: even when something does not exist, there is a sense in which it both can come to be, and in which it already could have.

184. Marking *holôs adunaton genesthai* as a quotation (280b11), as Heiberg does not here (however, cf. 315,4-5 below).

185. 313,17-314,14.

186. 314,17-21.

187. Compare Aristotle's acceptance of a loose sense of 'infinite', meaning 'capable of traverse, but with difficulty': *Phys*. 3.4, 204a5.

188. On contacts, and their instantaneous generation, see *Phys*. 6.6; and see R. Sorabji, 'Aristotle on the instant of change', in J. Barnes, M. Schofield and R. Sorabji (eds) *Articles on Aristotle 3: Metaphysics* (London, 1979).

189. Or 'corresponds'; here Simplicius probably begins reporting Alexander's view: see n. 192 below.

190. sc. although it will.

191. 'Swiftly' and 'well' are not found in this lemma, but Simplicius reasonably supplies them from the previous one (280b14); this is a close paraphrase, although not a direct citation, of 280b16-18.

192. It is not clear from our MSS just how much of the previous account Simplicius intends to ascribe to Alexander (and hence, following Heiberg, I have not marked any of it as a quotation) – but it seems plausible to suppose that all of the oppositions from 315,20 onwards are Alexander's; the text prior to 315,20 may be lacunose.

193. The adverb used is *philoponôs*; and it is conceivable that this is intended as an ironic pun on the name of his rival Philoponus.

194. 280b11-12.

195. i.e. whether or not there is any process of generation for it: compare 313,17-314,14 and 314,17-315,11.

196. These words, *mê einai*, were evidently missing from Simplicius' MSS: see below, 316,19-20: and n. 197; but they were read by Alexander: 317,24-6; n. 209.

197. Simplicius' MSS omitted the *mê einai* of our exemplars (see n. 196 above); Simplicius proposes supplying mentally *husteron mê einai*; the sense is the same.

198. 315,16-23.

199. i.e. the chaff is never actually separated (since the grain is never cut) although it might have been. That Aristotle does recognise such unactualised possibilities is clear from *Int.* 9, 19a13-14: a cloak is capable of being ripped even if it wears out naturally. Quite how this is to be squared with Aristotle's adherence to the Principle of Plenitude (see n. 89; and *Cael.* 1.12 *passim*) is another question. But in any case it seems that Simplicius' interpretation (that Aristotle is here referring to things which are destroyed but for which there is no process of destruction: cf. 280b15-16 above) is likely to be the correct one.

200. 280b15-16.

201. 325,29-31.

202. i.e. 'easily, swiftly, or well': 315,25.

203. 280b17-18.

204. 316,14-19.

205. Reading *adunaton* with c, for *dunaton* of the MSS of Simplicius here (which is also the reading of the majority of the MSS of Aristotle, and apparently of Alexander: 318,15; but see n. 214) in view of what Simplicius says below at 318,13-16.

206. i.e., this is the sense 'not yet destroyed', parallel to 'not yet generated': 280a9-11; 314,15-20 above.

207. This sentence has frequently been secluded by modern editors of Aristotle's text (Hayduck, Allan), it certainly seems out of place here (see Hankinson and Matthen, ad loc.); however, Simplicius clearly both read it and did not suspect it (318,29-319,1).

208. The sentences enclosed by '< ... >' (280b31-281a1) are omitted from the lemma. Heiberg remarks (app. crit. ad loc.) that they belong here (the next lemma, 319,6, begins after this at 281a1), and I have adopted this solution; but cf. n. 209 below.

209. i.e. to the end of the lemma as represented in the MSS of Simplicius, i.e. to 'or that these things are touching'; this perhaps suggests that another lemma should be added, containing the missing sentences of 280b31-281a4: see n. 208 above.

210. Alexander clearly reads the *mê einai* missing from Simplicius' MSS: above, nn. 196-7.

211. See n. 203 above.

212. sc. at some future time; Alexander in the previous clauses distinguishes once more between cases of instantaneous destruction and those where destruction is a process: see 280b6-9; 313,15-314,14.

213. 280b33-4.

214. This clause does not appear in the citation from Alexander quoted above (317,20-318,9); Simplicius may mean that Alexander evidently understood the text this way, or (perhaps more probably) that he actually did quote it thus in a passage not reproduced by Simplicius.

215. See n. 205 above.

216. i.e. given that this is the correct text.

217. The 'loose sense' is the non-modal sense of *aphthartos*, more naturally rendered in English as 'undestroyed'; but it is hard to capture the Greek ambiguity in English without awkwardness: see n. 3.

218. 316,14-25.

219. 315,16-23.

220. 315,24-5.

221. 280b25; 317,3-4.

222. It is just possible that this may refer to *Metaph.* 5.12, which deals with various senses of *dunatos*; but in all probability Simplicius means that the concepts of capability and incapability have already been made use of, but without explication, in the preceding discussion of the senses of 'generated', 'ungenerated', 'destructible', and 'indestructible'.

223. i.e. for walking exactly one hundred stades, lifting exactly one hundred talents.

224. i.e. the lesser amounts – e.g. the capacity to walk seventy stades.

225. i.e. capable of no more than this, in the sense defined.

226. At any rate counting in whole numbers: someone capable of walking only four stades and no more is presumably incapable of walking four and a quarter.

227. Heiberg, in his apparatus, cites *Laws* 10, 894A: but this is hardly pertinent; the references should be to 10, 902C.

228. i.e. the largest visible and audible objects will be grasped by any sense, no matter how weak.

229. 'The possible (*to dunaton*)' is an addition of Heiberg's – but it is clearly required, unless perhaps the text requires more serious surgery.

230. This sentence, the first of ch. 12, is omitted from Simplicius' lemma; moreover, Heiberg apparently places this lemma with ch. 11 (v. Heiberg, 1894, p. 322, header) – but this is surely a slip.

231. I translate *einai te kai mê einai* here, and in most other subsequent contexts in this chapter, as 'existing and not existing', rather than 'being and not being', following the practice already established, even though both Aristotle and Simplicius make it clear that what is being asserted applies to any of the categories; but I have mostly preferred the perspicuity of 'exist' over the generality (and archaism) of 'be'; and in any case, there is nothing particularly problematic about asserting the existence of properties, relations, etc.

232. The idea is that if something has the capacity for existing for an infinite time, then it must be possible for it to exist for ever; but if it is possible for it to exist for ever, and does so, then there can be no time for it not to exist, so it is not possible that it can not exist (and certainly not for ever). It is the job of the rest of this chapter to make good on these highly dubious modal claims (on which see Hankinson and Matthen, ad loc.; and S. Waterlow, *Passage and Possibility* (Oxford, 1982), esp. chs 2-4.

233. This argument is valid; but the question precisely is, why cannot something have existed for an infinite amount of past time, be destroyed now, and fail to exist for an infinite stretch of future time (if time is indeed infinite in both directions, as Aristotle supposes that it is: see below, 283a10; and *Phys.* 3.6, 206a9-11; 8, 208a519-20)? The rest of the chapter seeks to answer this question; see Matthen and Hankinson ad loc.

234. The words in brackets are not in our text of Aristotle, but it appears from the commentary that Simplicius read them (324,17-18; 324,27-30; cf. 323,11-15; 336,21; 337,2; 359,10-11), although the evidence is not conclusive (Simplicius may simply have been expanding the text for the sake of clarity); in any case, the sense is unaffected.

235. *An. Pr.* 1.15, 34a25-32. The claim is not that anything validly deduced from false premises will be false (or from impossible premises impossible), since Aristotle (and presumably Simplicius) was well aware that sometimes true conclusion can be validly deduced from false premises (*An. Pr.* 2.2-4; and since anything follows from an impossibility, the same thing goes in that case too); but rather that if a false conclusion is validly deduced, then one (at least) of the premises must be false; and similarly in the case of impossible conclusions; see n. 245 below.

236. i.e. than their sum; the claim is that on the hypothesis that the angle-sum of a triangle is 2R, it will be impossible for the external angle of a particular angle not to equal the sum of the other two internal angles. The example is not a particularly happy one of hypothetical *impossibility*, since of course it actually is the case (in Euclidian geometry at any rate, which was the only sort known to the ancients), that the angle-sum is (and is necessarily) 2R.

237. Reading *diplasia* for the MSS *diplasiôn*.

238. Omit *to de haplôs* with A.

239. These are examples of hypothetical truth and falsity, rather than necessity and possibility, because it is a contingent fact that it is now day; given the assumption that it is not, it follows of necessity (hypothetically) that it is night, but it does not follow as a necessary (hypothetical) truth; of course, as Simplicius goes on to point out, examples of hypothetical necessity and impossibility are also *ipso facto* respectively examples of hypothetical truth and falsehood: 323,30-324,9.

240. sc. the hypothetically true and false.

241. cf. n. 236 above.

242. This example casts some light on the nature of the modalities at issue: when I am swimming, it is not impossible for me to sit (i.e. the mere fact that I am not sitting does not render me incapable of sitting, ever again), although of course I cannot sit-while-swimming: cf. 281b12, and n. 239 above; and 324,15-16 below.

243. sc. in the future: Aristotle's capacities are forward-looking: see n. 242 above; and Hankinson and Matthen, ad loc.; and see 355,18-356,18 below; nn. 461, 466.

244. It is very hard to see what the bracketed clause could add to the passage quoted – it seems to say exactly the same thing in slightly different words, while the *oude* ('and nor') ought to introduce some genuinely new consideration rather than a mere exegesis (and it must be said that even if it is the latter it is spectacularly feeble). The words should probably be secluded, as they are in bc.

245. Simplicius should not mean that everything that follows from a falsehood is itself false, and everything that follows from an impossibility is impossible (trivially, since anything follows from an impossibility, including its negation); it is preferable, then, charitably to take him as meaning that it is possible that something false will follow from something false, and something impossible from something impossible: cf. *An. Pr.* 1.13, 32a18-20 (possibly the passage Simplicius has in mind): 'I call possibility and the possible that which is such that, while not being necessary, if it is assumed nothing impossible will follow' (see *Metaph.* 9.3, 1047a24-9; and cf. 4, 1047b3-4, 13-22, and *Int.* 13); see also *An. Pr.* 1.15, 34a6-33; 2.2-4; but 25-33 do indeed imply that all conclusions based on a false premiss (or conjunction of premisses) will be false; see n. 235 above.

246. The point is that while every capacity may be for a maximum (11, 281a7-27; 319,20-321,33), they need not be for a specific length of time; thus there may be a maximum length of time during which I can have grey hair, but my capacity for having grey hair is not a capacity for having it for precisely that length of time (forty years, say), such that if I die after being grey for only twenty years I will not have realised the capacity, and certainly not for having it at a particular time (1990-2030, say); see further n. 272 below.

247. The argument is the following: if a thing possesses contrary capacities, it possesses them in virtue of its being able to exercise them at different times. But if something were to possess capacities for the infinite exercise of two contrary capacities, there would be no time at which these capacities could be exercised – the actualisation of one contrary capacity would take up the whole of time, to the exclusion of any time for the actualisation for the other; see further 326,18-30.

248. i.e. (E) if, for all x, x is ungenerable if and only if x is indestructible, then if x is either ungenerable or indestructible, x is eternal (this is proved at 282a21-b14). Of course (E) only has a chance of being a theorem if the universal quantifiers have existential import (that is, the possibility of something's being trivially ungenerable and indestructible on the grounds of its never existing – and hence clearly not being eternal – needs to be ruled out: see 327,4 below); but universals for Aristotle (and other ancient logicians) standardly do have such import, as evidenced by the acceptance of the laws of subalternation (all As are Bs entails some As are Bs; and no As are Bs entails some As are not Bs: cf. *An. Pr.* 1.2, 25a5-25).

249. Because if for all x, x is destructible if and only if x is generable, then for all x, x is indestructible if and only if x is ungenerable.

250. In what follows Simplicius seems to advert to only two lines of reasoning, that leading from the eternal existence of both the ungenerable and of the indestructible to their mutual entailment, and that from their mutual entailment to their eternal existence; but he probably means to treat the argument which begins from the mutual entailment of the destructible and the generable to the mutual entailment of the indestructible and the ungenerable, and hence to their eternal existence, as a separate line of argument: see above, nn. 248-9.

251. See nn. 232, 247 above.

252. This is another expression of the fundamental modal principle in operation here which we may call the 'Capacity Principle', or CP: if something is genuinely possible, then no impossibility can result from the supposition that that possibility is actualised at some time; or rather, in these contexts, if x genuinely has the capacity for F-ness, no impossibility can follow from supposing that at some time x is F (which comes to the same thing); cf. *in Cael.* 1.10, 271b21-31; 302,13-21, nn. 90, 136-7; cf. *An. Pr.* 1.13, 32a18-20; n. 245 above; and see Hankinson and Matthen ad *Cael.* 281b18.

253. Perhaps read *phtharomenon* for *phtheiromenon*; the MSS present participle should rather have the sense 'suppose it to be being destroyed', which is not to the point here.

254. In other words, we should be able to make the (false) assumption that it does not exist at some particular time (this is the force of 'as it might be') without any impossible result following from it – otherwise the principle that what is impossible follows only from what is impossible will be violated: 326,32-3; and see nn. 245, 252.

255. i.e. it is implied by what he says.

256. See nn. 248 above, 257 below.

257. i.e. if something has the capacity of existing for an infinite time (as opposed to having for an infinite time the capacity for existing, or perhaps rather of being F for some value of F, since we have established that non-existents can have no capacities: 327,4; cf. 327,14-16), then by the Capacity Principle (nn. 245, 252; cf. n. 254) we should be able to assume that this capacity is realised without any impossibility resulting – but if it also has the capacity for not being, then, this capacity too must be instantiable consistently with the instantiability of its other capacities; but on the assumption that the capacity for infinite temporal existence is instantiated, then we cannot also assume the instantiation at any time of a capacity for non-existence without contradiction; see Hankinson and Matthen, ad loc.

258. 281b18-19.

259. 281b21-2. Alexander has Aristotle supposing that both of the capacities which are supposed to be realised are so for an infinite time.

260. In other words, Simplicius thinks that Aristotle can derive the result he needs simply by supposing that the object has the capacity for an infinite time for not being, since its having this capacity for an infinite time entails its existing for an infinite time (which Simplicius tacitly assimilates here to existing for ever; but see below, 283a10), so it will for ever exist, having the capacity to be destroyed; but since it has now been established to be an eternal existent, there can be no time at which it can be assumed (counterfactually) to exercise the capacity for non-existence without contradiction. The contradiction is generated on the assumption merely that the infinite existent has the capacity for not being *at some time*, rather than that it has the capacity for eternal non-existence; on Simplicius' view, Aristotle introduces the stronger thesis in the next lemma (281b25-33): see 328,8-23, below; but see Hankinson and Matthen ad loc.

261. i.e. for an infinite time.

262. i.e. is itself infinite [sc. in duration]: see n. 257 above.

263. Thus Simplicius takes *haplôs* here to mean 'unqualifiedly' in the sense of 'unconditionally', and this may be right; but Aristotle might rather mean to restrict the scope of 'indestructible' to the category of substantial existence: thus an eternal existent might have a capacity for being destroyed in respect of some property F (i.e. for ceasing to be F), although it is itself indestructible.

264. i.e. this argument is parallel to that regarding the capacity for destruction elucidated in the previous lemma.

265. i.e. it doesn't matter which period of time you suppose counterfactually it not to exist for: the supposition of its non-existence then will conflict with its eternal existence, and so it will violate CP (n. 252 above).

266. See n. 264 above.

267. i.e. suppose that the eternally existent x also possesses the capacity for being generated; if x is generated, then at some time x does not exist; but then, by CP (n. 252 above), we must be able to suppose that x does not exist at some time without contradiction. Let that time be t: but at t, x also exists; therefore, by CP, x both exists and does not exist at t, which is impossible; hence the

assumptions that generated that conclusion must themselves contain an impossibility.

268. 282b4-10; and see 328,26-329,1.

269. This is the likeliest meaning of the Greek, given the word-order; however, Simplicius ought to have said 'possesses the capacity for always not existing'.

270. i.e. if it is supposed counterfactually to be the case, in line with CP: n. 252 above.

271. Here Simplicius looks forward to the argument of the next lemma: 282a1-3; 329,25-9.

272. Simplicius' argument apparently relies on supposing that (1) to have a capacity for not existing for some time (as is entailed by the idea of something's being generable, since if it is to be generated it must at some time not exist) entails that (2) there is some particular stretch of time T for which it has that capacity; but in that case, (3) it would not, before or after that time, be generable; hence (4) it is not always generable (i.e. it does not always have the capacity for being generated at some time or other). Matters are complicated by the ambiguity of the Greek, which lacks explicit scope-operators. (1) pretty clearly does not entail (2) on any standard interpretation of modality, and there is no reason to think that Aristotle thought that it did. Moreover, the words that express (3) (328,26) might mean 'it would not be generable-before-or-after-that time': i.e., it would not have the capacity for being generated at times other than T, although it might, at other times, have the capacity for being generated at some time during T; but that of course does not yield the requisite conclusion. Further, if we suppose it not to exist only at T (but not that it only possessed the capacity for not existing at T), then we might, on Aristotelian grounds (capacities are forward-looking: see nn. 242-3), hold that after T it no longer had the capacity for non-existence, but not, as Simplicius holds, that it could not have had this capacity before. So Simplicius seems committed to (2), and it is difficult to discern any reasonably hopeful line of argument that might allow him to infer to it (and see n. 246 above); he was probably confused about scope here, and in more than one way (as indeed perhaps was Aristotle: but see Hankinson and Matthen ad loc. for an alternative interpretation).

273. Reading *einai dunasthai* with A in place of *dunasthai einai* (CE^2b, Heiberg – DE have only *dunasthai*); the reading preferred by Heiberg should rather translate 'it is not possible for one and the same thing both always to be capable of existing and always not to exist', which certainly makes sense (it would be an expression of the Principle of Plenitude: below, n. 276), but seems not to be the claim actually canvassed by Simplicius here.

274. This is the standard logical definition of contrariety: A and B are contraries just in case nothing A is B, but not everything that is not-A is not-B; other senses of contrariety are also important: see nn. 280, 298 below.

275. i.e., according to the doctrine of the atomists, the temporary agglomerations of atoms which form perishable objects.

276. Simplicius clearly interprets Aristotle's argument as depending on the thesis that 'destructible' and 'generable' both actually entail 'at some time does not exist' (i.e. that the Principle of Plenitude holds: see *in Cael.* 1.10, nn. 90, 136-7): cf. 329,25; 335,1-6 below; but it is not clear that he needs a thesis this strong either here or elsewhere, and a contradiction can be derived from the weaker principle I have called CP (above, nn. 252, 265, 267, 270).

277. i.e. that when one is true, the other is false and *vice versa*.

278. The idea is that if the verb-predicate 'is' has genuine temporal force, then negation will be achieved by prefixing the negation to the verb: 'Socrates is pale'; 'Socrates not is pale'; but if there is a temporal adverb (for instance) involved, the 'not' must prefix the adverb: 'Socrates is always pale'; 'Socrates is not always pale'. The examples are obviously artificial – and indeed the claim false – in English (but sense could be salvaged by talking instead, in such sentences at least, of the negation prefixing the predicate adjective); but in Greek what Simplicius says is generally true (at least if ambiguity is to be avoided, which is of course the whole point of such stipulations); and there clearly is a difference in English too between 'Socrates is not always pale' and the (admittedly rather artificial again) 'Socrates is always not pale'. On the distinction between propositional and predicate contrariety, see n. 307 below.

279. i.e., when we say, e.g., 'a diamond is for ever', the 'is', although grammatically in the present tense, does not limit the scope of the claim (evidently) to the present only.

280. Contraries 'are the furthest apart of things in the same genus ... or are such as to exhibit the greatest difference, either *simpliciter*, or generically, or specifically': *Metaph.* 5.10, 1018a26-31; cf. 10.4, 1055a3-5; see below, 332,4-6.

281. See n. 274 above.

282. See *Int.* 12, 21b10-22a13.

283. The Principle of Non-Contradiction, a corner-stone of Aristotle's logic, semantics, and metaphysics: *Metaph.* 4.3-6.

284. See n. 276 above.

285. i.e. by showing that this case, i.e. the relation between the generable and the destructible, is a special case of a general theorem, to the effect that if A is a necessary condition for B, and A cannot obtain, then B cannot obtain.

286. i.e. 'not always existing': Simplicius means that this is not really a distinct argument establishing that what always exists cannot be generable; rather that it cannot be generable depends upon the previous argument's having established by *reductio* that it cannot be destructible (on the grounds the destructibility entails that at some time it is not, and hence is not always), and the equivalence of destructibility and generability.

287. i.e. the general theorem supplies the reason why whatever holds in the case of the destructible will hold in the case of the generable too – and hence implicitly invokes the previous argument 'from the negation' involving destructibility.

288. Of course, since in Aristotle's (and Simplicius') view whatever is generable is also destructible, and *vice versa*, the claim cannot be that 'what sometimes is not' has a greater *extension* than 'the generable' in virtue of its also including 'the destructible' – rather the sense of the one includes the other.

289. See n. 286 above.

290. i.e. the supposition of Alexander and others that this is not a demonstration by way of negation; the reason is that Aristotle does not explicitly use a negation-operator here.

291. Or: 'belong to the same essence': this is just another way of saying that whatever has one has the other.

292. i.e. in the previous lemma.

293. This indicates that some at least of the previous stretch of exposition is to be attributed to Alexander – but it is unclear how much.

294. The expression is rather baroque: Simplicius means that if F and G are contradictory predicates, then everything is either F or G; the reference to negation is superfluous (presumably it simply means that everything will also be either not-F or not-G – which is true, but trivial).

295. i.e. between that which always exists and that which never exists.

296. Insert *kai to aei einai* after *dioti*.

297. The argument and the text are uncertain here. It appears that Alexander is here arguing only that anything which satisfies both (a) 'not always not existing' and (b) 'not always existing' will exist only for a certain period of time, and not that each of (a) and (b) do separately, and hence that they entail one another; and that indeed is all that he is entitled to argue: (a) is compatible with existing for ever, and (b) with never existing, and obviously nothing can satisfy both of those conditions. But the text Heiberg prints here after 'it follows that' (and no alternatives are reported in his apparatus), *hôste kai to mê aei mê on kai to mê aei on*, seems precisely to assert the mutual entailment thesis; it is possible that the text should be emended to read *hôste to mê aei mê on kai mê aei on*, which would yield the desired sense.

298. Alexander has in mind here contraries which taken together exhaust the domain in question, as his subsequent examples show; it is left to Simplicius to consider the case of non-polar opposite contraries, such as yellow and green. On unmediated and mediated contraries, see *Cat.* 10, 11b38-12a25; 12b26-13a17.

299. Reading *kaiper* for *epi gar*: Heiberg's text would translate 'for both are true in the case of wood', which gives the wrong sense: the fact that their negations *are* both true of something (even if this is case because neither the predicate nor its negation are appropriate for the subject in question) cannot provide a reason why there is no genuine intermediate between them. But this may be an intruded marginal note (perhaps even one of Simplicius' own, since he is going to disagree with this view of Alexander's: 332,6-16), since cases which are neither F nor not-F because the concept of F-ness simply has no application to them are not really to the point here. See also nn. 305, 313 below.

300. This paragraph gives Simplicius' own position, by contrast with that of Alexander which has occupied the previous stretch of text; see 333,25-6 below.

301. Herophilus indeed defined medicine as 'the science of things which are healthy, things which are diseased, and things which are neither' (T 43, von Staden, 1989; cf. T 42-8).

302. 'Even-odd' numbers are those even numbers which, when divided by 2, yield odd numbers (e.g. 6, 10, 14, etc.); 'odd-even' are those which yield an odd number when divided by a power of 2 (e.g. 24, which divided by 2^3 yields 3; it is hard to see how these examples establish Simplicius' point here, since they are evidently types of even number.

303. See n. 280 above.

304. See nn. 298-9 above.

305. i.e. something defined by the holding of the negations of the contraries 'always existing' and 'always not existing' will indeed be intermediate between the contraries in the strong sense, since it must exist at some time: it is not always existent and not always not existent: a point (for example) is not white and not black (or non-white), but it is not the case that it is not always white and not always not white. This is the point made in the subsequent paragraph (see nn. 299 above; 313 below).

306. i.e. the terms are simply predicates, and not predicates conjoined with subjects to make complete sentences.

307. On propositional contrariety, see *Int.* 7, 17b3-6; 10, 20a16-23: 'No As are Bs' is the contrary of 'All As are Bs'; cf. n. 278 above.

308. On these alleged Aristotelian modal equivalences, see J. Hintikka, 'Necessity, universality and time in Aristotle', *Ajatus* 20 (1957), 65-90; and Waterlow (1982), 49-77.

309. The point is that polar contrariety is officially defined as being maximum opposition within the same genus (above, n. 280; 322,4-5) thus black and white are maximally opposed in the genus of colour. But there can be no genus common to things which always exist and things which never do. Alexander's suggested reply is perhaps possible, but it would have been preferable in this case to determine the 'genus' as that of temporal existence.

310. sc. this general capacity for being and not being.

311. i.e. dummy letters which stand proxy for any term (as in 'all As are Bs'): one of Aristotle's greatest contributions to rigour and generality of logical argument.

312. Reading *tis* for *ho ti*: the text printed by Heiberg would translate: 'having first determined that the argument is general', and it is hard to see what that would add in the context.

313. i.e. a contradictory opposition has the form 'F & not-F': hence everything is either F or not-F; the rigour of the argument is somewhat compromised by the fact that it is terms and their negations which are being treated of, rather than propositions (for which for Aristotle and classical logic the principle that one or other of p and not-p must be true – the Law of Excluded Middle – holds: *Metaph.* 4.7; and 333,20-1 below), and as was noted above, in cases where the predicate could not conceivably apply to its subject neither it nor its opposite are predicable of the subject, and so what might be termed the 'Predicate Law of Excluded Middle' ('everything is either F or not-F but not both') fails to hold (cf. *Int.* 7, 10); but this is easily amended: 'everything for which it is possible to predicate F is either F or not-F but not both'; see nn. 299, 305 above; and Alexander, 333,24-334,1 below.

314. Simplicius' language suggests that A and B are themselves to be read as propositional variables – but this cannot be right (see n. 313 above); rather he is thinking of the propositions formed by concatenating them with a subject-variable: 'x is A' is the contrary of 'x is B'.

315. If $(x)((\neg Ax \to Cx) \& (\neg Bx \to Dx))$, then $((\exists y)(\neg Ay$ and $\neg By) \to (Cy$ and $Dy))$. This is indeed a theorem; but see Hankinson and Matthen ad 282a14.

316. See 331,26-34 above.

317. 282a13-14.

318. 282a4-12.

319. sc. that it always exists: the subject of the argument is 'what always exists': 334,10.

320. This explanatory clause hardly seems to give the right reason why, if we assume that what always exists is generable and destructible too, we will be committed to contradiction: rather it is simply because on Aristotle's view 'generable' (and 'destructible') entail not always existing that, if what always exists is generable, it must also not always exist.

321. This clause, which is hard to make sense of in the context, is probably to be secluded as an intrusion.

322. The contradiction is, according to Alexander, arrived at by the Capacity Principle: nn. 252, 265, 267, 270 above; and see further nn. 324, 326 below. Simplicius demurs: 335,1-13, and n. 327 below.

323. See 281b2-20; 322,21-325,3 above.

324. sc. that what is capable of not existing does not exist: this is false (since by hypothesis we are dealing with an eternal, albeit generable, object) but it should not be impossible (otherwise it cannot be said to have the capacity at all, and we are supposing it to be generable); if such an object is possible, then by CP we should be able to suppose that it exists without generating a contradiction: but since it is by hypothesis eternal, it cannot be supposed at any time not to exist without generating a contradiction; so what generates the contradiction (and hence is impossible) is not the hypothesis that what is capable of not existing does not exist, but rather that there could be something exhibiting both the characteristics of eternal existence and of generability.

325. Simplicius' text omits both 'always's of Aristotle, and it is assumed by some editors (e.g. Moraux) that neither Simplicius' nor Alexander's MSS had 'always' here. But the first of them is clearly required by the sense (although the second is not); and the point the commentators are making here simply concerns the notion of capacity; hence they may very well have ignored the 'always', even though it was read in their MSS.

326. i.e. Alexander focuses on the consequences of supposing an eternal object to possess this capacity, and derives the contradiction therefrom.

327. i.e. in respect of the same predicate: there will be some time at which x is both F and not-F, for some value of F. Simplicius then, contrary to Alexander (above, n. 322), supposes Aristotle simply to rely on the Principle of Plenitude (*in Cael.* 1.10, nn. 319, 365-6; and n. 276 above): if x has the capacity for not-F, then at some time x will be not-F – but since it is F all the time (by hypothesis) this generates a contradiction.

328. i.e. it is not merely *potentially* non-existent (which is all that is required by the CP-argument): at some time it actually will be non-existent (by PP: *in Cael.* 1.10, n. 90).

329. i.e. in the case where he uses the expression 'capable of being'.

330. i.e. merely potentially and not actually.

331. sc. at different particular times.

332. *amesos*, a technical term in Aristotle's demonstrative theory as outlined in *An. Post.*; a proposition is unmediated (or immediate) just in case it is not derivable from further true propositions which are prior to it; unmediated propositions are thus axioms of the system (*An. Post.* 1.2, 72a7-8, 14-16; although Aristotle himself calls them posits, reserving the term *axiôma* for 'that which must be grasped if anything is to be learned', i.e. such basic principles as that of non-contradiction: 72a16-17).

333. *Tim.* 41A-B; this is not of course Simplicius' own interpretation of the passage: see 1.10, 294,7-10 (nn. 253-4); and especially 296,1-301,18.

334. i.e. the mutual entailment.

335. Again, not that it necessarily lasts for a particular length of time: above, nn. 246, 272.

336. The two second-figure syllogisms can be constructed as follows. (1) Everything indestructible is eternal; nothing generated is eternal; so nothing generated is indestructible (a syllogism in Camestres). (2) Nothing destructible is eternal; everything ungenerated is eternal; so nothing ungenerated is destructible (a syllogism in Cesare).

337. Inserting *to* before *aphtharton*.

338. Reading *to phtharton* with D.

339. Or perhaps: 'of that which is completely non-existent, i.e. that which is not capable of coming to be'; it is hard to see how the completely non-existent is supposed to differ from that which is not capable of coming to be, unless perhaps in that in the latter case there is *something*, namely the diagonal, and what cannot happen is that some property comes to hold true of it; but it is hard to see what that distinction would achieve.

340. i.e. of a square: cf. 1.12, 281b8; 323,20-325,3 above.

341. cf. 1.11, 280b6-9; 313,20-7 above.

342. i.e. this clause appears in Alexander's report of the lemma.

343. Simplicius supposes that Alexander must read 'eternal' instead of 'indestructible' in the second clause, since he speaks of adding 'and existent' 'to each of them' – and the best candidates for 'each of them' are 'eternal and ungenerated' in the next clause; but it is surely preferable to think that Alexander does mean by 'each of them' the ungenerated and the indestructible, and is simply here speaking of one of them in place of both, and adding 'eternal' to it (since as we now know, the ungenerated and indestructible is eternal: 282a25-6; and a30-b7 below).

344. Reading *tôi de* with c, against *to de* of the MSS.

345. Reading *to de* with c, against *tôi de* of the MSS.

346. To correspond to 'since it is either destructible or indestructible': 282b1-2.

347. Reading *tou phthartou* here, with JHE[4], in light of 340,15 below.

348. See above, 282a4-22; 330,19-334,20.

349. See above, n. 296: there is no obvious, non-question-begging reason to suppose that what does not always exist must always not exist as well, and *vice versa*; but Simplicius rather supposes that it already has been established that there is an intermediate between these two, and that it will be both generable and destructible, although again such an argument must rely on physical rather than logical considerations: logically, something ungenerated but destructible or generated but indestructible will also be intermediate between these two extremes. See further below, 341,5-344,27; esp. 342,2-32.

350. Again, this does not immediately follow, without the possibility of something's coming into being at some time and continuing for ever (or the reverse) having been ruled out, since any such object will exist for an infinite (and hence not a determinate) time, albeit one which is infinite in only one direction. But of course, Simplicius does take Aristotle to have established the convertibility of ungenerability and indestructibility; and he will go on to endorse Aristotle's arguments against one-way (or 'semi-bounded': see n. 367 below) infinities (below, 283a10; 347,24-30), even though he allows that such infinite times, if they were to exist, would not be determinate.

351. 1.12, 282a9, above.

352. Simplicius seems to err here in treating 'generated' as the contradictory of what always is (and equally in the case of the destructible), although it is true that what is generable will not always be, and equally that what is destructible will not always not be; again, see nn. 349-50 above.

353. This is the interpretation of most commentators; but it seems more probable that Aristotle means by the two limits that which exhausts the whole of time and that which occupies no time at all: see Hankinson and Matthen ad loc.

354. Given that, for Aristotle, properly speaking capacities are forward-looking (above, nn. 242-3, 272), this consideration seems irrelevant; see n. 370 below; and 355,18-356,18: nn. 461, 466 below.

355. i.e. existent or non-existent.

356. i.e. when actually existing it is potentially non-existent, and *vice versa*.

357. See 328,8-14 above: nn. 252, 267; cf. 322,21-325,28.

358. Reading *hêi* with c for *ei* of the MSS.

359. See nn. 235, 245 above.

360. By CP: nn. 252, 265, 267, 270, 276, 324 above.

361. 282b20-1.

362. See n. 350 above.

363. 330,29-334,20.

364. i.e. it is not the case that something is red if and only if it is yellow; on the senses of contrariety, see nn. 274, 280, 298 above.

365. i.e. everything intermediate between these extremes has the same defining property, that of temporary existence (the fact that their particular

durations may be different is in this sense an accidental feature of them); hence they form a unified class, as being things definitionally equivalent, and not merely sharing some definitional properties (unlike, e.g., red and yellow, which are not the same, although they are both, and definitionally, colours: n. 364 above).

366. i.e. 'generable' means 'capable of not being at some *earlier* time', while 'destructible' means 'capable of not being at some *later* time'); hence even though each definition refers to a time of possible not being, they do not yet necessarily coincide (see n. 349 above); the whole of the rest of the discussion of this lemma (down to 344,27) seeks to address this issue.

367. By 'determinate in both directions' Simplicius means finite (as opposed to being bounded at one end only, or 'semi-bounded'); but it is hard to see how, given an infinity of time, this can be the case. If something exists only for a determinate, finite stretch of time, say from t_1 to t_2, then presumably it fails to exist for a semi-bounded infinite stretch of time prior to t_1, and for another semi-bounded infinite stretch of time to t_2, unless it has a discontinuous, recurrent existence. But in that case it is hard to avoid the conclusion that the totality of its time of existence is infinite, as is that of its non-existence (although such a conclusion would certainly not be welcome to Aristotle, and indeed similar spatial considerations underlie his rejection of the possibility of infinite spatial extension: see *Phys.* 3.5, 204a20-34).

368. i.e. of always existing and always not existing.

369. See above, 338,18-339,14; and n. 349.

370. Here Simplicius does treat the capacities as forward-looking: 'generable [sc. from now on]' is indeed equivalent to 'not always non-existent [sc. in the future]', just as 'destructible [sc. from now on]' is equivalent to 'not always existent [sc. in the future]'; see n. 354 above.

371. i.e. prior to actually being F it had the capacity for being F; or, alternatively: 'it comes to be this from something which had the capacity [for being this]'.

372. i.e. the thing in question, prior to being F was not-F – and hence it must still have the capacity for being not-F; but if it has that capacity then it will at some future time be not-F (by PP: n. 90 above).

373. All these contentions rely on the fact that capacities are capacities of the material – and since the material does not change through the changes (definitionally), neither will the capacities; see 354,22-355,4: n. 459 below.

374. See n. 349 above.

375. Perhaps add *khronon* after *apeiron*; but the sense could equally well be supplied from the context.

376. i.e., in accordance with the doctrine of temporal maxima (*in Cael.* 1.11, 319,20-320,6), there must be an upper limit on the length of time for which anything generable may exist: but this is incompatible with its existing for an infinite future time (see further nn. 350, 367 above).

377. i.e. in the direction of the future: it is true to say of the generated but indestructible object (such as the world of the *Timaeus*) that it exists for ever (i.e. from now on), but not of course that it *has existed* for ever; but in that case we need only distinguish between the two different senses of 'for ever' in order to refurbish the objection.

378. 282b20-1.

379. i.e. a particular mass of fire; see further below, 344,22.

380. For the implicit conditions of identity operative here, see *in Cael.* 1.10, 293,16-18; 308,25-8: n. 360.

381. Alexander's argument requires not merely that the underlying matter is *capable* of changing into different things at different times, but that it *will* do so – or rather, that numerically the same thing will never be recreated from the same matter. By the same token, what matters for the argument is not that the matter can be informed by different types of form (now a man, now a horse, as it might be), but rather that even if it does take on the same type of form (e.g. Socrates' matter later becomes that of Bertrand Russell), still that form must be numerically distinct from any other token of that type which the matter has previously constituted (or will subsequently constitute): see further 344,5-27 below.

382. i.e. it is bounded at both ends, unlike the time for its future non-existence after a contingent thing's destruction.

383. i.e. it does not exhaust the whole of infinite time; although it is without end.

384. e.g. air and water, although not at opposite poles of the elemental spectrum, are still contraries in the logical sense that their predications cannot be true of the same thing at the same time, although their negations can both be false of the same thing (n. 274 above). The doctrine that all change is between contraries is fundamental to Aristotle's account of change: cf. *Phys.* 1.7; 5.1, 224b26-225a20; 5.5, 229a7-b21; 5.6, 230a7-231a4.

385. It was widely believed in antiquity (although not apparently by Aristotle: *HA* 5.23) that wasps were generated from rotting horse-flesh: see e.g. Sextus Empiricus, *Outlines of Pyrrhonism* 1.41.

386. By 'body' here Simplicius probably means 'parcel of elemental stuff'; but it is not clear what this is supposed to add to the claim about matter in the previous clause.

387. The point is that, given that we can track the same parcels of matter through various changes, and given that, in time, the same matter will coalesce once again into the same form, then even composites will have a determinate (i.e. non-infinite, even one-way infinite) time for their non-existence, since they will inevitably recur again (and again) after finite intervals of time. This presupposes that objects can have a discontinuous existence, which is not of course uncontroversial: cf. 1.10, nn. 7-8, 130-4; and see n. 381 above.

388. It does not seem necessary that the co-extensiveness of generability and destructibility should be proved prior to that of ungenerability and indestructibility, since they will follow logically from one another; but perhaps Simplicius supposes that 'generable' and 'destructible', being positive and not privative terms, are prior to the others. On the other hand, from a metaphysical point of view, one might suppose ungenerability and indestructibility to be the prior pair, in the manner in which Aristotle supposes actuality to be prior to potentiality (*Metaph.* 9.8; and see nn. 390, 429 below).

389. This is true only if 'ungenerable' is read as 'not capable of generation', and hence can apply not only to things which exist without any process of generation or things which cannot as a matter of fact be generated, but also to things for which the notion of generation itself makes no sense: only then will the disjunction be exhaustive.

390. i.e. it is not simply equivalent to 'not generated': see nn. 388-9 above.

391. *An. Pr.* 2.22, 68a4-15; Aristotle there actually uses as an example the relations between generable and destructible, ungenerable and indestructible to illustrate the general point.

392. Above, 326,14-16; 330,21-9; 334,23-336,11.

393. Simplicius treats of the implication in this direction (from indestructibility to ungenerability) rather than its converse because, although the terms are co-extensive and hence biconditionally related, the crucial point at issue is

still the hypothesis of the *Timaeus* (41A-B), where the actual indestructibility of the world is supposed to be compatible with its having been generated; see further below, 346,16-29.

394. 'Follow from' is a trifle too strong for *akolouthein* here, the sense being closer to 'be consistent with' (cf. 300,29-301,1 above); the idea is not that it is a logical truth that if indestructibility does not entail ungenerability, then it must *entail* generability – it might (logically) entail neither. But at least then generability will be compatible with indestructibility – but since generability has been shown to imply destructibility (above, 330,21-9; 334,23-336,11), then it cannot be so compatible (this is the *reductio* promised by Simplicius: 345,14).

395. Here again, more strictly 'will be consistent with'.

396. 345,1-11.

397. i.e. that the ungenerable does not follow from the indestructible.

398. Reading *tôi E*, with Eb, for *to E* of ADE^2, as printed by Heiberg.

399. Simplicius conceives of the argument as involving syllogisms in the second figure mood Cesare: (1) nothing destructible is eternal; everything ungenerable is eternal; so nothing ungenerable is destructible; (2) everything indestructible is eternal; nothing generable is eternal; so nothing generable is indestructible.

400. The reference is to *Cael.* 1.3, 270a12-b4, where Aristotle argues that since all generation and destruction are from and to contraries (cf. *Phys.* 1.5-8), while the heavenly element has no contrary, it cannot suffer destruction; other 'physical arguments' are offered at 1.10, 279b12-280a27, in summary of which at 280a32-4, Aristotle claims only to have refuted the *Timaeus* doctrine and others 'in physical terms', and promises to continue in a more general vein: (see above, 312,23-8); cf. 1.12, 283b17.

401. *Timaeus* 41B.

402. *in Cael.* 1.10, 311,27-31; Simplicius disagrees with the interpretation: 311,31-312,6.

403. i.e. the argument will be a *reductio*.

404. In the previously-quoted sentence: this inferential particle indicates that it is this (namely that everything which can act or be affected can be so either for a finite or an infinite time), which is the assumption which is imperiled by the opposition's argument; Alexander effectively treats the remarks about the capacities for action and affection as introducing new, unrelated considerations.

405. The consequent of the conditional (that there cannot be something which is generated but indestructible or ungenerated but destructible) is suppressed here.

406. However, see the remarks of Alexander and Simplicius above, 343,29-344,1.

407. This apparently conflicts with the seminal Aristotelian dictum that the infinite 'is the opposite of what people say it is; it is not that of which no part is outside, but rather that of which there is always something [of itself] outside that is infinite .... So the infinite is that of which, if a certain quantity is taken, there will always be something outside it to take' (*Phys.* 3.6, 206b33-207a8). But Aristotle's point there is that the way to grasp infinity is in terms of iteration – it is that which is always greater than any finite quantity. Simplicius' point here is simply that there is no time not comprehended by an infinity of time, and that in that sense it is complete and whole, where completeness and wholeness are defined for Aristotle as 'that of which there is nothing more outside' them (3.6, 207a9-10); cf. *Metaph.* 5.16, 1012b14-16: 'in one sense we say that what is complete is that outside of which not even one part can be found, as for instance the complete time of each thing is that outside which no time can be found which is part of that time'. The next few lines make this clear.

408. Aristotle excludes the possibility of there being actualised infinite collections of things, preferring to treat the infinite instead as an inexhaustible potential: *Phys.* 3.5-6, esp. 6, 206a9-207a32; and this analysis is explicitly applied to the case of time in *Phys.* 4.13, 222a28-b7.

409. *Phys.* 3.5; and see nn. 407-8 above.

410. cf. Aristotle's definition of the infinite: above, n. 407.

411. The one-way (or semi-bounded) infinite: see nn. 350, 367, 387.

412. sc. a genuinely (and not one-way) infinite time.

413. 'Nows' are present moments: cf. *Phys.* 4.11, 219a10-33; of course, since time is continuous and 'nows' are punctual, there is an infinite number of them in any finite stretch of time as well (cf. 4.12, 220a4-26), the implications of which Aristotle struggled to swallow within the limits of his finitist mathematics: see *Phys.* 3.7, esp. 207b27-34; and see Hussey, 1983 ad loc., and pp. 178-9.

414. Here Simplicius following Aristotle, appeals to the Principle of Sufficient Reason (PSR), first perhaps employed in such contexts by Parmenides (28 B 8.9-10): 'and what need would have impelled it later or earlier to be, coming from nothing?'; cf. *in Cael.* 1.10, nn. 98, 138.

415. Another invocation of the fundamental modal principle CP: see nn. 252, 265, 267, 270-1, 324 above; but it appears rather as though the argument requires PP (*in Cael.* 1.10, n. 90): see below, n. 418.

416. See above, 322,21-325,28.

417. The parenthesis is logically superfluous given the commutativity of conjunction, and it is tempting to seclude it as an intruded (and rather fatuous) marginal gloss; but the difference of ordering is meant to distinguish between the case of (a) something which has existed for an infinite amount of time and then is destroyed, and (b) something which has been non-existent for an infinite time and then comes to be. The first conjunct expresses the background condition of actuality which is held constant during the process of modal testing, while the second refers to the possibility which is supposed hypothetically to be actualised against that background.

418. i.e., since an impossibility (rather than simply a falsehood) followed from the supposition in question, the supposition cannot have been merely false, but must have been impossible too: see nn. 235, 245 above. Note that the supposed impossibility is not generated by CP (above, n. 415), since it is not the case that there is *no* time available in which the infinite previous existent can be assumed to be destroyed or the infinite previous non-existent to be generated, since *ex hypothesi* they *are* destroyed or generated, now (but see 283b6-14, 355,18-356,18 below, on forward-looking capacities). Rather the argument must invoke PP: in an infinity of past time, throughout all of which (by PSR: n. 414) the objects must be supposed to possess the capacities in question (in the case of the prior non-existent, the Pickwickian 'object' is the material from which it will be generated: see n. 466 below), still the capacity has not been realised – but there could be nothing to prevent it from being realised for an infinity of time.

419. *skopos*: the term has the connotation of 'goal', 'target': i.e. this the point of the argument, what it basically aims to achieve.

420. Aristotle's text at 283a12 does indeed omit the word for time (*khronon*); but that is very frequently taken as understood in such contexts.

421. So Simplicius treats the word *apeiron* here as adverbial (effectively as an accusative of respect); but it seems that Alexander's explanation is the more likely, hence my translation of the lemma.

422. *sêmeia*, literally 'signs' (cf. 348,24 above); *sêmeion* has the geometrical sense of 'point', and Aristotle here extends its usage to cover temporal points, or instants; at *Phys.* 4.12, 224a9-20 Aristotle applies the more or less equivalent *stigmê* to time.

423. cf. *Phys.* 6.6. Coming to be in this sense is instantaneous: i.e. there is a moment at which something can truly be said to have come (wholly) to be, and prior to which it cannot (although given the density of the temporal continuum, if there is a first moment of complete existence, there will be no last moment of generation: see Sorabji, 1979). This is quite compatible with certain sorts of comings to be being temporally-extended processes.

424. Simplicius makes this suggestion because in the previous lines (283a13-14) Aristotle has concentrated on what we should say about the infinity of past time that has elapsed, in the case of the thing destroyed of past existence and of the thing generated of past non-existence, and he supposes that Aristotle should continue to be concerned with this here, in which case what has been generated was, prior to its generation, capable *of existing* for an infinite period of time – and indeed that would give Aristotle a neater argument. But it is clear from the subsequent lines (283a14-17) that in the case of the thing generated he is considering its future career (perhaps because he has qualms about referring to the capacities of as-yet-non-existent objects: cf. n. 418 above; but see 283a20-4, and n. 440 below), and throughout that infinite time it will, while existing, possess the capacity for non-existence for an infinite time (since, given that it *has been* generated, its materials possessed the capacity for generation, and since they have not changed, they must still possess it: see 342,2-12, nn. 371-3 above; 354,22-355,4, n. 459, below). Thus Simplicius' suggestion of ellipsis should be rejected; 283a20-4 supply this line of argument.

425. i.e. for some determinate finite period of time.

426. i.e. at every instant ('now') the postulated object will either exist in actuality (and trivially potentiality: but see 350,20-1; n. 430 below) and not exist in potentiality, or not exist in actuality (and trivially potentiality) and exist in potentiality; but then we can run the Capacity Principle indifferently for any of the instants (by PSR) and obtain a contradiction; and hence, by PSR, if we can suppose the contradiction instantiated at any instant we can suppose it so at all instants; see further below, 350,31-351,7.

427. See n. 413 above.

428. This phrase, which is found in all the MSS of Aristotle, is secluded by Allan, Guthrie and Moraux; and it is indeed somewhat confusing for the argument in view of the fact that it would have to mean a one-way infinite time, while the same expression at the end of the lemma clearly refers to the whole, complete temporal infinity; however, Simplicius apparently read it here (350,21-2.25-6; 351,11-12 below).

429. Precedes in a temporal sense; elsewhere Aristotle is at pains to distinguish the temporal precedence of the potential from the metaphysical priority of the actual: *Metaph.* 9.8, 1049b4-27; cf. 12.6, 1071b22-6; 12.7, 1073a1-3; and see n. 388 above.

430. And hence the potential in the strict sense is not yet actual.

431. See n. 428 above.

432. At *Cael.* 1.11, 280b9-11; 314,17-20.

433. Simplicius suggests that the first clause (Aristotle's) somehow implies the second, which is a rather strong claim; but his point is that, in saying that the existence of the potentiality for the whole period of its prior non-existence entails that it will have the capacity for all time, he does imply that it will have the capacity during the time of its existence too.

434. Simplicius again invokes PSR (see nn. 414, 418, 426 above) in this paragraph, to generate the conclusion that the object not only possessed for an infinite time the capacity for being but rather that it possessed the capacity of being-for-an-infinite-time; but it is hard to see how it can really underwrite the move from 'possible at any time' to 'possible at all times'.

435. sc. the generable and the destructible.

436. 1.12, 283a24-9; 351,15-352,33.

437. Most MSS of Aristotle (endorsed by modern editors) have *kai aphtharton* here; but it is clear that Alexander's MSS did not read it, and nor did the bulk of those available to Simplicius: see below, 352,13-23. The preferred modern text might also translate: 'for it will always be both at the same time destructible and indestructible in reality'.

438. *Tim.* 41A-B; cf. 346,22-3 above.

439. *Tim.* 41B.

440. See above, nn. 418, 424.

441. Alexander does not read the *kai aphtharton* of most surviving MSS of Aristotle (at 283a25-6) which yields the sense translated; and he also reads a *kai* before *hama*. Cf. 352,22-3 below; and n. 437 above.

442. Thus Alexander extracts implicitly from the passage the sense which it explicitly has according to the preferred modern reading: n. 437 above.

443. However, see the suggested translation in n. 437 above.

444. Reading *kath' ho* for *kath' hous* (*kath' hou* D).

445. *in Cael.* 1.10, 296,1-30, esp. 6-8, 26-30.

446. *Tim.* 37D-38B.

447. 'Perceptible and corporeal': *Tim.* 28B-C, 31B. 'What is really real': *Tim.* 28; *Laws* 10, 894A; the concept figures largely in Simplicius' disquisition on Neoplatonist metaphysics at *in Cael.* 1.3, 92,33-107,24, esp. 96,29-105,2. 'Has its being in becoming': cf. *Tim.* 27D-29D, 51E-52B; *Phil.* 53C-54D; *Theaet.* 152D-E; and *in Cael.* 1.10, 297,12: n. 47; 298,24; etc.

448. cf. *in Cael.* 1.10, 301,1-7: n. 80; cf. n. 482 below.

449. *Tim.* 41B; Simplicius' text of Plato differs, although not significantly, from ours.

450. *Phys.* 8.10.

451. i.e., since all destruction is *ipso facto* generation of something else, the world which is destructible but perpetually undestroyed will, in virtue of its unrealised capacity of destruction, also possess an unrealised capacity for the generation of what would have come from it were it destroyed (compare Alexander's earlier claim that what is generated but indestructible entails the existence of something – the unformed matter from which it was created – which is ungenerated but destroyed: *in Cael.* 1.10, 310,27-31; n. 161). But Aristotle seems rather to be arguing that, since the destructible is also generable, hence it will have been generated, and hence will not always have existed (so Guthrie, 1936, 125 n. b); alternatively he may (harshly) be referring to another object which is generable, which is how Alexander himself takes it (353,16-21; and so does Moraux, 1965, 52).

452. 331,29-332,26.

453. Or perhaps: 'grip', as in wrestling-hold, here (obviously) used metaphorically (see LSJ, s.v.).

454. At *Phys.* 2.4-6 (esp. 5-6, 196b17-197b19), Aristotle distinguishes between the results of chance (*to automaton*) and of luck (*tukhê*); broadly, the latter consist of that subset of chance outcomes which follow on intentional action and are such that they might have (although they in fact did not) come about as a result of deliberation directed towards the outcome as such (thus they are the unforeseen results of actions undertaken for other reasons). But this technical distinction is not relevant here, and the expression for both Aristotle and Simplicius is probably pleonastic.

455. This is not obviously the case: Simplicius leaves out of account those things that come to be as a result of deliberation and voluntary agency; and in this case this is no casual omission, since the perpetual preservation of the cosmos by demiurgic *fiat* presumably would fall under just this heading.

456. On the association of what is natural with what occurs always or for the most part, and the distinction of such things from chance (and rare) events, see *Metaph.* 6.2, 1026b27-32; *Phys.* 2.8, 198b34-199a4; *An. Post.* 1.30.

457. It is hard to see why this should be thought to be the case, since if the whole span of time is infinite, then the span of anything which begins to exist at some time and then continues for ever (and equally that of one which has always existed but stops existing at some time) will be of the same size as the span of its non-existence.

458. In Camestres: everything everlasting is so either always or for the most part; no matter of chance is so either always or for the most part; therefore nothing everlasting is a matter of chance.

459. And hence if something was generable (prior to its generation) it cannot now not be generable (and hence be indestructible); or rather if something had the capacity for non-existence prior to its generation, it must still possess that capacity, since that capacity must have been natural (and hence essential) for it; see nn. 371-3, 424 above.

460. Simplicius reports MSS reading 'it does not exist last year' (below, 355,29), and later he comes down in favour of it (356,13-14 below; n. 467); but this reading is printed by all modern editors, and Simplicius seems to prefer it here.

461. For this doctrine of 'forward-looking capacities', see Hankinson and Matthen, ad 283b6-14; and see nn. 242-3, 272, 354, 370; for the sort of option it is intended to forestall, see n. 418 above.

462. i.e. there is a discrepancy in the MSS at this point: see nn. 460 above, 467 below.

463. i.e. what goes for one time cannot be assumed also to be true for another. But while it is obviously true that nothing is now existing last year, it cannot follow from that that nothing which now exists *was* existing last year; and it is hard to see what real work this talk of time and tense can do for Aristotle here: see Hankinson and Matthen ad loc.

464. i.e. although when it exists it possesses the capacity for not-existing (a capacity in virtue of its possibly not existing *at some other time*), it does not possess the complex capacity for not-existing-when-it-actually-exists: (1) at t, (Ex and $\diamond \neg Ex$), is true, but (2) at t, $\diamond(Ex$ and $\neg Ex)$, is not.

465. i.e. if it is made (by divine fiat) indestructible at t, then it will turn out, after t, retroactively always to have been indestructible; but this seems to be true only in the sense that it will never in fact be destroyed, not that it could not have been destroyed.

466. Relying on the intuitively plausible principle that if at t, x has the capacity for F, then x must exist at F; and while earlier arguments may seem to have undermined that principle (see n. 418 above), none the less a weaker analogue (if there is a capacity at t for x's being F, then the materials for x must exist at t), which is compatible with the earlier considerations, will still suffice to do the trick here.

467. i.e. at 283b7: see nn. 460, 462 above; but there is no real reason on the basis of what Aristotle writes here later to prefer this reading in the earlier passage, where he is making a perfectly general point about time and tense.

468. For the doctrine of the necessity of the past, see *Rhet.* 3.17, 1418a3-5; *EN* 6.2, 1139b7-9; it is discussed by J. Hintikka, *Time and Necessity* (Oxford, 1973), ch. 9.

469. Not of course literally everlasting, but having existed for an infinite period of past time: see 358,18-26.

470. i.e., since the object is by hypothesis destroyed for all future time, then we cannot suppose without contradiction that it is destructible in the sense that it will be destroyed once more in the future, since that entails that it will again exist in the future, which is incompatible with the supposition that it has been destroyed without hope of revival. But then, if it is to possess the capacity for destruction (which it must do in virtue of its matter), it will have to do so in respect of past time: but we have already seen that that is impossible (nn. 461, 466 above). Simplicius' construal of the argument is rendered needlessly complex by his concentrating on future destructibility rather than future generability.

471. In other words, since it must always have the capacity for existing (since this is natural for it: above, 354,23-355,4; 357,2-3), and since this capacity must be forward-looking, no absurdity should result from supposing this capacity exercised in the future (by CP: n. 252 above); but in that case it cannot have been irrevocably destroyed.

472. 1.10, 280a32-4; 312,14-28: nn. 396-7.

473. *GC* 1.2-3; 'will demonstrate', since Simplicius sees Aristotle's *oeuvre* as an ordered whole in which *Cael.* precedes *GC*: see *in Cael.* Proem, 2,27-3,2.

474. *Cael.* 1.3, 270a26-35.

475. *Phys.* 1.5.

476. *Cael.* 1.3, 270a13-23.

477. 283b1-2; 354,11-22.

478. 283a4-5.

479. *Tim.* 41A-B.

480. Here Alexander omits a clause from his quotation, an omission for which Simplicius will upbraid him: 362,8-13.

481. *Theaet.* 176A; Heiberg wrongly ends the quotation after 'this place'.

482. Alexander might also have noted *Tim.* 37D: 'and just as this [i.e. the perfect being] was an eternal animal, he tried to make the universe of such a nature, as far as possible. But the nature of the animal happens to be eternal, and it was not possible to join this completely to something generated'.

483. On God's lack of enviousness, see *Tim.* 29D-30A.

484. *Phys.* 8.6-10; cf. n. 448 above.

485. Simplicius' point is that the heaven receives from the Prime Mover a power of infinite movement (movement without cessation), although it is itself limited in extent and hence not a subject of infinite powers; his main idea is, presumably, that if left to itself (i.e. absent the Prime Mover) the heaven would not rotate for ever; and hence it is in a sense eternally mobile only by the dispensation of some higher power, and so (in a sense) potentially limited in movement even though it will not, as a matter of fact, ever be so limited. This is supposed to parallel the *Timaeus* case, and hence if Aristotle allows one he should allow the other; but in fact the parallel is not precise: the heaven never has, as a matter of fact, not moved (and hence it is possible for Aristotle to maintain that it is necessarily and eternally mobile); while, at any rate on the temporal reading, the *Timaeus* world has at some time not existed. But of course Simplicius himself rejects that reading in favour of the metaphysical depend-

ence interpretation (see *in Cael.* 1.10, 294,7-10; 296,1-301,28); and this will allow him to restore the parallelism between the cases.

486. Simplicius means that Plato said it was generated by God, while Aristotle holds that it is primarily moved by God: the Greek is ambiguous in the same way as my English translation.

487. *Pol.* 272e-273e; Simplicius also refers to it at *in Cael.* 1.10, 303,19-24.

488. Perhaps, in place of *tou skhêmatos* ('its figure') read *tôn skhêmatôn* ('its figures') here, referring to the different structures that the corporeal takes on to become each of the four elements (cf. *Tim.* 48E-55C); of course, Simplicius does not think, unlike Christians such as Philoponus whom he abominates, that God actually creates matter itself: cf. *in Cael.* 1.3, 137,21-8.

489. Read *kai theia kath' hauta* for *kai kath' hauta* (I am indebted to an anonymous reader for this elegant suggestion).

490. Reading *endidomenês* with A in place of *endidomena*; i.e. the generation of corporeal form is itself a divine thing, the production of the Demiurge; but even more divine is the Demiurge's gift of eternal existence to his creations: cf. *Tim.* 29D-41D.

491. Reading *hôsei* for *ei* at 361,8: this clause is difficult to parse in the context, and there is trouble with the text hereabouts; it should perhaps be secluded.

492. sc. by divine dispensation.

493. i.e. to treat as separated conceptually things which cannot as a matter of fact be separated.

494. At this point, our Greek MSS break off: the rest of the chapter is preserved in William of Moerbeke's thirteenth-century Latin translation, of which the *editio princeps* of Aldus Manutius (Venice, 1526), is a Greek retroversion: see Heiberg, app. crit. ad loc., and Praefatio, p. x.

495. Above, 360,1-3.

496. i.e. a good and an evil principle, along gnostic or Manichaean lines. As he goes on to make clear, Simplicius follows the standard Neoplatonic line that the evils of the material world consist fundamentally in privations of goodness, and do not subsist in their own right.

497. The reference is to *Metaph.* 12.10, 1076a4 (cf. *Pol.* 4.4, 1292b13), where Aristotle objects to the multiplicity of governing principles invoked by Speusippus and the Pythagoreans; Aristotle is himself quoting Homer (*Il.* 2.204): the line is completed by the clause 'let one be the ruler'.

498. *Theaet.* 176A: this is indeed omitted from Alexander's citation above (359,24-6); see n. 481.

499. The privation of form being, in the Neoplatonic scheme of things, evil: cf. Plotinus I 8.

500. i.e. if God had chosen not to create the sublunary realm at all, there would have been no evil; but he chose to do so, with the inevitable result that evil was created, since he desired to create the type of goods which such a world expresses (and which, it is supposed, outweigh the evils). Here Simplicius adopts the language of divine voluntarism which would not have been uncongenial to his Christian opponents; and he seems to be some distance removed from the standard Neoplatonic conception of the goodness of the One simply spontaneously overflowing into the being of the lower realms of reality. However, compare Proclus, *On the Subsistence of Evils* 10, 188-91 Boese, referring to *Tim.* 30A.

501. i.e. terrestrial animals, whose bodies are composed of complex mixtures of the four elements (as opposed to the divine animals, the heavenly bodies) – since they are so composed, their composition is liable to dissolution.

502. i.e. the terrestrial composite ones.

503. The point is that man is defined (among other things) by his mortality: an immortal man is a contradiction in terms. So if God were to make everything incorruptible, he would do so at the expense of not creating man at all – and Simplicius relies on the intuition that it was better to create a necessarily imperfect species than not to create it at all; hence the destruction of evil would in fact entail a greater evil (his moves here bear some resemblance to contemporary 'personal identity theodicies', as well as to more traditional theological approaches to 'the problem of evil').

504. This exordium is typical of Simplicius' evidently deep and sincere pagan religious feeling. See Hankinson 2002a, Introduction.

Select Bibliography

Arnim, H. von (1903-5) *Stoicorum Veterum Fragmenta* [= *SVF*], 3 vols (Leipzig); vol. 4, indexes, by M. Adler, 1924
Barnes, J. (1979) *The Presocratic Philosophers*, 2 vols (London)
Blumenthal, H.J. (1978) '529 and its sequel: What happened to the Academy?' *Byzantium* 48, 369-85, and reprinted in his 1993
Blumenthal, H.J. (1979) 'Themistius, the last Peripatetic commentator on Aristotle?' in G.W. Bowersock, W. Burkert and M.C.J. Putnam (eds) *Arktouros*, Hellenic Studies presented to Bernard M.W. Knox (Berlin & New York) 168-82
Blumenthal, H.J. (1993) *Soul and the Intellect* (Aldershot)
Boese, H. (1960) *Procli Diadochi Tria Opuscula (De providentia, libertate, malo). Latine Guilelmo de Moerbeka vertente et Graece ex Isaacii Sebastocratoris aliorumque scriptis collecta* (Quellen und Studien zur Geschichte der Philosophie 1) (Berlin)
Broadie, S. (2001) 'Que fait le premier moteur d'Aristote?', *Revue Philosophique* 183, 375-411
Cameron, A. (1969) 'The last days of the Academy at Athens', *Proceedings of the Cambridge Philological Society* 195, n.s. 15, 7-29
Charlton, W. (1970) *Aristotle: Physics I and II*, Clarendon Aristotle Series (Oxford)
Dicks, D.R. (1970) *Early Greek Astronomy to Aristotle* (Ithaca, NY)
Diels, H. and Kranz, W. (1951^6) *Die Fragmente der Vorsokratiker* [= DK], 3 vols (Berlin)
Dillon, J.M. (1973) *Iamblichi Chalcidensis in Platonis Dialogos Commentariorum Fragmenta* (Leiden)
Dodds, E.R. (1951) *The Greeks and the Irrational* (California)
Foulkes, P. (1992) 'Where was Simplicius?', *Journal of Hellenic Studies* 112
Frantz, A. (1975) 'Pagan philosophers in Christian Athens', *Proceedings of the American Philological Society* 119, 29-38
Frede, M. (1985) 'Substance in Aristotle's *Metaphysics*', in A. Gotthelf (ed.) *Aristotle on Nature and Living Things* (Bristol/Pittsburgh), repr. in Frede, 1987
Frede, M. (1987) *Essays in Ancient Philosophy* (Oxford/Minnesota)
Glucker, J. (1978) *Antiochus and the Late Academy* (*Hypomnemata* 56) (Göttingen)
Guthrie, W.K.C. (1936) *Aristotle: On the Heavens*, Loeb Classical Library (London & Cambridge MA)
Haas, F. de (1997) *John Philoponus' New Definition of Prime Matter* (Leiden)
Haase, W. and Temporini, H. (eds) *Aufstieg und Niedergang der Römischen Welt* [= *ANRW*] (Berlin/New York)

Hadot, I. (1969) 'Die Widerlegung des Manichäismus im Epiktetkommentar des Simplikios', *Archiv für Geschichte der Philosophie* 50, 46
Hadot, I. (1996) *Simplicius: Commentaire sur le Manuel d'Epictète* (Leiden)
Hadot, I. (ed.) (1987) *Simplicius – sa vie, son oeuvre, sa survie*, Peripatoi vol. 15 (Berlin)
Hadot, P. (1990) 'The life and works of Simplicius in Greek and Arabic sources', in Sorabji, 1990
Hankinson, R.J. (1988) 'Stoicism, science and divination', in R.J. Hankinson (ed.) *Method, Medicine and Metaphysics* (*Apeiron* Supp. Vol. 21)
Hankinson, R.J. (1998) *Cause and Explanation in the Ancient Greek World* (Oxford)
Hankinson, R.J. (2002a) *Simplicius: On Aristotle On the Heavens 1.1-4* (London & Ithaca, NY)
Hankinson, R.J. (2002b) 'Xenarchus, Alexander and Simplicius on simple motions, bodies and magnitudes', *Bulletin of the Institute for Classical Studies*
Hankinson, R.J. (2003) *Simplicius: On Aristotle On the Heavens 1.5-9* (London & Ithaca, NY)
Hankinson, R.J. (forthcoming a) 'Mathematics and physics in Aristotle's theory of the ether', in C. Wildberg and A. Bowen (eds) *Essays on Aristotle's De Caelo*
Hankinson, R.J. (forthcoming b) 'Natural, unnatural, and supernatural motions: contrariety and the argument for the elements in *de Caelo* 1.2-4'
Hankinson, R.J. and Matthen, M. (forthcoming c) *Aristotle: On the Heavens I*, Clarendon Aristotle Series (Oxford)
Heiberg, I.L. (1894) *Simplicii in Aristotelis de Caelo Commentaria* (Berlin), *Commentaria in Aristotelem Graeca* [= *CAG*], vol. VII
Hintikka, J. (1957) 'Necessity, universality and time in Aristotle', *Ajatus* 20, 65-90
Hintikka, J. (1973) *Time and Necessity* (Oxford)
Hoffmann, P. (1987) 'Simplicius' polemics', in Sorabji, 1987
Hussey, E. (1983) *Aristotle's Physics Books III and IV*, Clarendon Aristotle Series (Oxford)
Isnardi Parente, M. (1980) *Speusippo: Frammenti* (Naples)
Isnardi Parente, M. (1982) *Senocrate, Ermodoro: Frammenti* (Naples)
Kirk, G.S., Raven, J.E. and Schofield, M. (1983^2) *The Presocratic Philosophers* [= KRS] (Cambridge)
Lameer, J. (1997) 'From Alexandria to Baghdad: reflections on the genesis of a problematical tradition', in G. Endress and R. Kruk (eds) *The Ancient Traditions in Christian and Islamic Hellenism* (Leiden)
Larsen, D.G. (1972) *Jamblique de Chalcis, Exégète et Philosophe* (Aarhus)
Long, A.A. (1982) 'Astrology: arguments pro and contra', in J. Barnes, J. Brunschwig, M.F. Burnyeat, M. Schofield (eds) *Science and Speculation* (Cambridge)
Long, A.A. and Sedley, D.N. (1987) *The Hellenistic Philosophers* [= LS], 2 vols (Cambridge)
Matthen, M. and Hankinson, R.J. (1993) 'Aristotle on the form of the Universe', *Synthese* 96 3, 417-35
Moraux, P. (1965) *Aristote: Du Ciel*, Budé (Paris)
Moraux, P. (1984) *Der Aristotelismus bei den Griechen*, vol. 2 (Berlin)
Mourelatos, A.P.D. (1981) 'Pre-Socratic origins of the principle that there are no origins of nothing', *Journal of Philosophy* 78, 649-65
Rashad, M. (1997) 'A "new" text of Alexander on the soul's motion', in R.R.K. Sorabji (ed.) *Aristotle and After*, BICS supp. vol. 68

Select Bibliography

Riet, S. van (1991) 'A propos de la biographie de Simplicius', *Rev. Phil. de Louv.* 89, 506-14

Robinson, R. (1953^2) *Plato's Earlier Dialectic* (Oxford)

Robinson, R. (1969) *Essays in Greek Philosophy* (Oxford)

Ross, W.D. (1936) *Aristotle: Physics* (Oxford)

Ross, W.D. (1949) *Aristotle's Prior and Posterior Analytics* (Oxford)

Solmsen, F. (1960) *Aristotle's System of the Physical World: A Comparison with his Predecessors* (Ithaca, NY)

Sorabji, R.R.K. (1979) 'Aristotle on the instant of change', in J. Barnes, M. Schofield and R. Sorabji (eds) *Articles on Aristotle 3: Metaphysics* (London)

Sorabji, R.R.K. (1982) *Time, Creation and the Continuum* (London & Ithaca, NY)

Sorabji, R.R.K. (ed.) (1987) *Philoponus and the Rejection of Aristotelian Science* (London & Ithaca, NY)

Sorabji, R.R.K. (1988) *Matter, Space, and Motion* (London & Ithaca, NY)

Sorabji, R.R.K. (ed.) (1990) *Aristotle Transformed* (London & Ithaca, NY)

Staden, H. von (1989) *Herophilus: The Art of Medicine in Early Alexandria* (Cambridge)

Tardieu, M. (1986) 'Témoins orientaux du *Premier Alcibiade* à Harrân et à Nag 'Hammâdi', *Journal Asiatique* 127

Tardieu, M. (1986) 'Sâbiens coraniques et "Sâbiens" de Harrân', *Journal Asiatique* 274, 1-44

Tardieu, M. (1987) 'Les calendriers en usage à Harrân d'après les sources arabes et le commentaire de Simplicius à la *Physique* d'Aristote', in Hadot, 1987

Tricot, J. (1949) *Aristoteles: Traité du Ciel* (Paris)

Verrycken, K. (1990) 'The development of Philoponus' thought and its chronology', in Sorabji, 1990

Waterlow, S. (1982) *Passage and Possibility: A Study of Aristotle's Modal Concepts* (Oxford)

Wehrli, F. (1967-9^2) *Die Schule des Aristoteles: Texte und Kommentare* (Basel/Stuttgart)

Wildberg, C. (1987) *Philoponus: Against Aristotle on the Eternity of the World* (London & Ithaca, NY)

Wildberg, C. (1988) *John Philoponus' Criticism of Aristotle's Theory of Ether* (Berlin & New York)

Williams, C.J.F. (1982) *Aristotle: On Generation and Corruption*, Clarendon Aristotle Series (Oxford)

Wolff, M. (1988) 'Philoponus and the rise of pre-classical dynamics', in Sorabji, 1987

English-Greek Glossary

account: *logos*
activity: *energeia*
actuality: *energeia*
adduce: *epagein*
affirmation: *kataphasis*
air: *aêr*
alter: *alloioun*
alterable: *alloiôtos*
alteration: *alloiôsis*
animal: *zôion*
argue: *epagein*
argument: *epikheirêma, logos*
assume: *lambanein*
assumption: *dedomenon*
atom: *atomos*
axiom: *axiôma*

beginning: *arkhê*
body: *sôma*
bring up: *epagein*

capable: *dunatos*
capacity: *dunamis*
cause: *aitia, aition*
chance: *automaton*
change: *metabolê*
change, to: *metaballein*
circular motion: *kuklôi kinêsis*
circumference: *periphora*
commensurable: *summetros*
composite: *sunthetos*
composition: *sustasis*
concatenation: *sumplokê*
concave: *koilos*
conclude: *epagein*
configuration: *skhêmatismos*
confirmation: *pistis*
consistent with, be: *akolouthein*
contact: *haphê*
contradiction: *antiphasis*
contradictory: *antikeimenon*

contradictory opposition: *antiphasis*
contrariety: *enantiôsis*
contrary: *enantios*
conversion: *antistrophê*
convert: *antistrephein*
convex: *kurtos*
corporeal: *sômatikos, sômatoeidês*
cosmic ordering: *diakosmêsis*

definition: *horismos*
Demiurge: *dêmiourgos*
demonstrate: *apodeiknunai*
demonstration: *apodeixis*
destroyed, to be: *apollusthai, phtheiresthai*
destroyed: *phthartos*
destructible: *phthartos*
destruction: *phthora*
determinate: *hôrismenos*
determined: *aphôrismenos*
diagram: *diagramma*
difficulty: *aporia*
directly: *prosekhôs*
discrimination: *diakrisis*
disorder: *ataxia*
disorderly: *ataktos*
disorderly fashion, in: *ataktôs*
disposition: *diathesis*
dissolution: *dialusis*
dissolve: *dialuein*
dissolved, to be: *luesthai*
distance: *apokhê, diastêma*
distinction: *diastolê*
divine body: *theion sôma*
divine: *theios*
division: *diairesis*

earth: *gê*
element: *stoikheion*
end: *telos*
entailment: *akolouthia*

eternal: *aïdios*
ether: *aithêr*
everlasting: *aïdios*
example: *paradeigma*
excess: *huperbolê*
exemplar: *paradeigma*
existence: *hupostasis*
explain: *didaskein*
expound: *exêgeisthai*
extension: *paratasis*
extremity: *eskhaton*

false, the: *pseudos, to*
false: *pseudês*
figure: *skhêma*
finite: *peperasmenos*
fire: *pur*
follow from, to: *akolouthein*
form, production of: *eidopoiia*
form: *eidos*
formula: *logos*
function: *khreia*

generable: *genêtos*
generated: *genêtos*
generation: *genesis*
genus: *genos*
get rid of: *anairein*
God: *theos*

hearing: *akoê*
heaven: *ouranos*
hypothesis: *hupothesis*
hypothetical: *ex hupotheseôs*

immobile: *akinêtos*
immobile cause: *akinêton aition*
immortal: *athanatos*
impossible: *adunatos*
incapable: *adunatos*
incommensurable: *asummetros*
indestructible: *aphthartos*
induction: *epagôgê*
infer: *epagein*
infinite: *apeiros*
infinity: *apeiria*
intelligible: *noêtos*
intermediate: *meson, metaxu*
investigate: *zêtein*
irregular: *plêmmelês*

letter: *stoikheion*
lightness: *kouphotês*

limit: *peras, telos*
limited: *peperasmenos*
Love: *Philos*
luck: *tukhê*

magnitude: *megethos*
matter: *hulê*
maximum: *huperokhê*
method of reasoning: *ephodos*
middle: *meson*
mode: *tropos*
motion: *kinêsis*
move: *pheresthai*
moving cause: *kinoun aition*

natural motion: *kinêsis kata phusin,
   kinêsis phusikê*
natural principles: *phusikai arkhai*
natural scientist: *phusikos*
nature: *phusis*
negation: *apophasis*
number: *arithmos*

objection: *enstasis*
obtain at the same time:
   sunuparkhein
opposing: *antikeimenon*
opposite: *antikeimenon*
order: *taxis*
ordering: *taxis*
origin: *arkhê*

part: *meros*
participate: *metekhein*
participation: *methexis*
particle: *morion*
passage: *lexis*
perceptible: *aisthêtos*
physical body: *phusikon sôma*
pick out: *ektithesthai*
plane: *epipedon*
point: *sêmeion*
posit: *tithenai*
possible: *dunatos*
potentiality: *dunamis*
potentially: *dunamei*
premiss: *hêgoumenon*
principle: *arkhê*
produce: *poiein*
productive cause: *poiêtikon aition,
   poiêtikê aitia*
proposition: *protasis*
putting together: *sunkrisis*

quality: *poiotês*

reality: *entelekheia*
reason: *aitia, aition*
reciprocally entail: *antakolouthein*
recur: *anakamptein*
recurrence: *epanodos*
responsible: *aitios*
revolving: *kuklophorêtikos*

said in many ways: *pollakhôs legesthai*
self-subsistence: *hupostasis*
sense: *aisthêsis*
separate, to: *diakrinein*
shape: *morphê*
sight: *horasis, opsis*
simple body: *haploun sôma*
simple: *haplos*
simpliciter: *haplôs*
smell: *osphrêsis*
solution: *euporia*
state: *hexis*
strictly speaking: *kuriôs*
Strife: *Neikos*
subject: *skopos*
substance: *ousia*
substrate: *hupokeimenon*
suppose: *hupotithenai*
supposition: *hupothesis*

tangible: *haptos*
temporal extension: *paratasis*
theologian: *theologos*
time: *khronos*
totality: *pan*
transformation: *hupallagê*
true, the: *alêthes, to*
true, to be at the same time: *sunalêtheuein*

unaffectible: *apathês*
unalterable: *analloiôtos*
undestroyed: *aphthartos*
ungenerable: *agenêtos*
ungenerated: *agenêtos*
unification: *henôsis*
unified: *hênômenos*
universe: *kosmos*
unlimited: *apeiros*
unmediated: *amesos*
usefulness: *khreia*

visible: *horatos*
visual: *horatikos*
void: *kenon*

water: *hudôr*
weight: *baros*
whole: *holon*
wisdom: *sophia*
world: *kosmos*

Greek-English Index

References are to the page and line numbers of Heiberg's *CAG* edition of 1894, which appear in the margin of the translation.

adunatos, impossible, 302,2; 303,5; 308,29; 315,5-10; 322,12; incapable, 314,21-315,10; 315,26-316,7; 318,16-18; 319,7-322,17; 322,21-360,17
aer, air, 304,18; 306,2.6
agenêtos, ungenerated, 292,10-15; 297,18; 298,13-14; 302,19; 309,15-18; 311,2-312,27; 312,31; 313,17-315,11; 315,14; 316,6; 319,6.11; 322,14-358,16; ungenerable, 314,28-315,10; 319,12-16; 326,1-358,18
aidios, eternal, 293,14.19; 301,16-18; 303,5-11; 307,19; 309,16; 312,11; 315,1; 325,31-326,34; 334,25.30; 335,33-337,9; 337,16-24; 338,9-10; 343,25; 344,16-20.30-1; 346,2-7.17-18; 351,25-6; 352,16.26; 353,8; 354,16; 355,7-14; 357,21; everlasting, 356,24; 357,22; 358,14-22
aisthêsis, sense, 320,11-321,29
aisthêtos, perceptible, 294,11; 296,13.18; 298,31; 320,13.32; 321,12.22; 352,32
aitia, reason, 293,6; 298,11-13; 301,25; 303,26-9; 309,30; 310,1.4; cause, 294,8; 299,30; 301,3.7; 361,4
aition, cause, 303,28; 308,14-16; 312,14.24; 354,10; reason, 330,16
aitios, responsible, 360,29; 361,5
akinêton aition, immobile cause, 353,8; 360,8-9
akinêtos, immobile, 290,3.29
akoê, hearing, 320,16; 321,10
akolouthein, be consistent with, 300,29-301,1; follow from, 326,3-32; 330,27-9; 336,5-11; 337,16-338,7; 338,21-8; 340,20.29; 343,27; 345,12-346,1
akolouthia, entailment, 338,3-6; 338,17
alêthês, to, the true, 329,8
alloiôsis, alteration, 294,25.31; 295,24-6; 306,13; 307,19; 308,4; 310,20.29
alloiôtos, alterable, 357,25; 358,8-15
alloioun, alter, 357,25; 358,1.9
amesos, unmediated, 331,28-332,6; 335,21
anairein, get rid of, 298,7; 331,18.26; 332,18; 338,31; 347,7.15
anakamptein, recur, 293,17-18; 310,3-311,19; 343,20; 344,27
analloiôtos, unalterable, 357,27-8
antakolouthein, reciprocally entail, 326,6-14; 336,10; 338,13-16; 340,20-34; 341,4.12; 342,12; 343,1; 344,32-345,18; 346,16; 347,1
antikeimenon, opposite, opposing, 325,16-28; 349,8-10; 352,11; 355,8; 355,19-24; 356,26; 359,4-9; contradictory, 345,3
antiphasis, contradiction, 329,2-3; contradictory opposition, 333,16-18
antistrephein, convert, 312,6; 326,1; 333,8-9; 334,24; 353,27
antistrophê, conversion, 312,4; 335,26
apathês, unaffectible, 294,31
apeiria, infinity, 310,31; 311,6

apeiros, infinite, unlimited, 294,29; 295,2-4; 308,30; 309,5.25; 310,1-30; 311,9-18; 313,25; 314,8; 322,7; 340,13; 342,22; 343,32-5; 344,18
aphôrismenos, determined, 329,16
aphthartos, indestructible, 292,11-14; 296,5.29; 298,4-14; 300,12-30; 301,23.32; 302,17-31; 304,3.16; 305,18-20; 307,16; 311,3-312,27; 312,31; 316,13-317,15; 317,21-318,21; 319,3-16; 322,12-360,2; undestroyed, 298,6; 318,5-11.21; 336,24; 356,2
apodeiknumi, demonstrate, 313,27; 353,5
apodeixis, demonstration, 292,21-32; 301,25; 325,10; 330,11-15; 333,12; 335,19.24; 338,22; 342,20; 345,15; 346,8-11; 354,7; 357,14.29; 358,6-7
apollusthai, be destroyed, 297,14; 300.9-11
apophasis, negation, 328,32; 329,5-330,17; 330,31-332,22; 333,1-334,18; 338,18-339,11; 340,23-341,30; 342,14-15; 353,25
aporia, difficulty, 292,21-3.30; 321,21; 341,20.33; 342,20.27
arithmos, number, 310,17; 344,8-26
arkhê, principle, 304,19; 306,1; 357,15-18; beginning, 292,26; 296,25; 297,21-3; 298,10-12.24; 299,3.6.15-30; 300,3; 301,27-35; 302,6.12; 303,16; 304,10.12.21; 307,1; 313,28; 326,33; 346,3; 347,26; 348,1; 354,15; 358,19; origin, 298,13; 301,4
asummetros, incommensurable, 323,7
ataktos, disorderly, 303,23.34; 304,32; 305,9; 311,32; 312,11
ataktôs, in a disorderly fashion, 304,2; 306,28; 311,33
ataxia, disorder, 303,21; 304,3; 305,9; 306,17-307,8; 311,29; 312,7; 360,32
athanatos, immortal, 353,4; 359,1; 360,11
atomos, atom, 293,17; 294,31; 295,23; 310,16-18; 311,5; 328,29
automaton, chance, 354,10-22

axiôma, axiom, 300,1.4; 301,35; 335,23; 357,23

baros, weight, 319,26-7; 320,26.29; 359,8

dedomenon, assumption, 346,28-348,10
dêmiourgos, Demiurge, 303,21; 306,27; 346,22; 351,17; 353,5; 360,32; 361,3
didaskein, expound, 313,1; 316,10; 336,30; explain, 324,10
diagramma, diagram, 303,32; 304,10-305,2
diairesis, division, 312,4; 313,6-13; 316,13-14; 317,21.28; 318,5
diakosmêsis, cosmic ordering, 294,19-20; 308,19; 360,30
diakrinein, separate, 293,22; 294,11
diakrisis, discrimination, 294,12; 295,21-3
dialuein, dissolve, 302,12-18
dialusis, dissolution, 310,5-28
diastêma, distance, 321,9-12
diastolê, distinction, 319,10
diathesis, disposition, 307,13; 308,22; 310,23; 344,22
dunamei, potentially, 302,1.5; 339,19-340,12; 350,20; 351,24; 352,12
dunamis, capacity, 301,5.35; 302,3-303,2; 309,1-14; 310,6; 312,13; 319,21-322,16; 322,22; 341,6-25; 342,4-9; 348,20-349,11; 350,4-5; 350,14-351,13; 351,28; 352,7-17; 353,3-10; 354,24-355,13; 355,18-356,17; 356,23-357,7; 359,12; potentiality, 350,18-20
dunatos, capable, 316,24-7; 317,5-6; 318,16; 319,7-322,11; possible, 323,14-324,14; 328,32-329,1; 342,14; 356,18.30; 359,30

eidopoiia, production of form, 306,21-5
eidos, form, 294,30; 295,25; 301,12; 305,19; 306,10.20.23; 307,21; 308,11.14; 310,14.17; 314,4; 344,8-27
ektithesthai, pick out, 315,16.30; 317,9

Greek-English Index

enantion, contrary, 292,20-7; 310,23; 312,17-25; 316,22; 325,13; 328,15.28.31; 329,18; 331,4-334,15; 339,6; 340,28-32; 341,18; 344,3-5.23; 346,10; 354,26; 358,1-16; 359,2
enantiôsis, contrariety, 357,29
energeia, actuality, 302,5.14.25; 325,12-25; 326,18-26; 335,7-12; 339,18-340,12; 347,14-19; 348,28; 349,3; 350,4-9; 350,18-351,4; 351,24-352,17; 354,7-9; 355,7-11; 355,24; 356,4.9; activity, 361,3; 362,14
enstasis, objection, 296,27; 305,26; 320,20; 347,30; 355,19.24
entelekheia, reality, 351,21; 352,1-22
epagein, argue, 299,23; 308,30; 311,25; 325,4; 330,14; 333,23; infer, 327,30; 328,8.30; 329,25; 334,8; 337,31; 338,1-2; 339,28; 340,9-17; 353,22; 360,14-15; adduce, 293,6; 311,22; conclude, 299,25; 310,3; 318,21; 341,20; 343,21; 352,24; 353,11; bring up, 293,11
epagôgê, induction, 301,24.31
epanodos, recurrence, 310,8
ephodos, method of reasoning, 326,11-12; 327,29
epikheirêma, argument, 329,5.29; 341,20; 348,14; 349,19; 350,13; 351,10-11
epipedon, plane, 304,15
eskhaton, extremity, 319,30
euporia, solution, 292,30
ex hupotheseôs, hypothetical, hypothetically, 304,4-307,9; 322,27-325,2
exêgeisthai, expound, 316,3

gê, earth, 304,19
genesis, generation, 294,9-295,24; 296,3; 297,15,21; 298,4.26; 300,26; 304,4.18.28.33; 305,6-33; 306,3; 308,4; 309,8-12; 310,21; 312,24; 313,19-314,1; 314,22; 315,17; 336,23; 342,4; 343,6.23.27; 344,18; 352,31; 357,24-6; 358,19
genêtos, generated, 292,13; 293,15; 294,26; 296,12-298,9; 298,23; 302,18-31; 304,16; 305,17; 307,15-16; 309,22; 310,27; 315,7; 315,14-316,8; 316,21-317,5; 319,6; 322,12-361,8; generable, 298,30; 300,12-28; 304,3.23; 308,25; 309,22; 311,14-15; 312,5-27; 312,30; 315,17-30; 326,6-16; 328,1-360,11
genos, genus, 332,24-33

haphê, contact, 313,21.27; 315,18; 316,17; 317,1.10; 318,21
haplos, simple, 304,12.20; 305,11-306,11; 361,1
haplôs, simpliciter, 324,10.16; 325,5; 327,18-5; 332,21-5; 333,25; 351,1; 354,15; 358,25; 359,5-8.19; 360,17; 361,12
haploun sôma, simple body, 344,2-6
haptos, tangible, 298,28
hêgoumenon, premiss, 302,11
hênômenos, unified, 294,10
henôsis, unification, 294,13
holon, whole, 296,15; 308,20; 347,22
horasis, sight, 320,16
horatikos, visual, 321,10
horatos, visible, 298,28; 304,1; 311,31-4
hôrismenos, determinate, 322,7; 328,20; 338,32; 339,8-18; 340,10-18; 341,1-7.24; 342,1.23-5; 343,2-344,24; 347,11-348,4
horismos, definition, 337,23; 340,17; 341,13
hudôr, water, 304,18; 306,1.6; 344,22
hulê, matter, 306,10.20; 307,20; 308,16.31; 310,24; 343,17-18; 344,18; 354,26-355,2
hupallagê, transformation, 307,27
huperbolê, excess, 319,31-320,2; 321,25-8
huperokhê, maximum, 319,21.30; 320,1.21.27; 321,22.32
hupokeimenon, substrate, 344,3; 354,24; 355,14; 356,26
hupostasis, existence, 296,14.20; self-subsistence, 360,28
hupothesis, hypothesis, supposition, 301,33; 302,10; 303,23; 310,9.27; 312,1; 325,1; 326,27.32; 330,29-32; 334,13, see also ex hupotheseôs
hupotithenai, suppose, 329,4;

330,29-34; 348,17-18; 349,5.7;
350,6-10; 355,5.10.12; 357,5-9

kataphasis, affirmation, 329,1.5.9;
331,4-16; 332,33; 333,17-20
kenon, void, 295,4.10
khreia, function, 292,17
khronos, time, 296,19-28; 297,24;
298,4-10; 299,16-21; 300,13-29;
301,12.23; 302,6-31; 303,16.26;
304,33; 305,1; 309,5.26; 312,9;
314,12; 322,7-15; 322,21;
325,13.17; 326,34; 327,7-13;
328,20; 329,9-15; 335,32;
339,1-27; 340,10-18; 341,2-7.24;
342,1; 343,2-344,25; 346,5;
347,9-348,4; 348,11-351,7;
352,29-31; 354,14; 355,25-356,5
kinêsis kata phusin, kinêsis phusikê, natural motion, 312,20
kinoun aition, moving cause, 312,13-14
koilos, concave, 295,17
kosmos, world, 292,10.22; 293,12-24;
294,4-295,28; 296,11.25;
297,14-25; 298,15-17; 299,4.9.11;
301,10.23.33; 302,6-27; 303,8-25;
304,21; 305,7-8; 307,5.16.20;
306,7-17; 307,14-312,15; 346,21;
351,19; 352,26-32; 353,5; 354,4;
355,5; 359,29-30; 360,32;
361,8-16; universe, 281,13-26
khreia, usefulness, 312,32
khronos, time, 313,30; 314,12;
321,30; 322,7-15; 322,21; 324,16;
325,13.17; 326,18.33; 327,6-13;
327,30-328,4; 329,9-15
kuklôi kinêsis, circular motion, 312,19-21
kuklophorêtikos, revolving, 312,22; 361,2
kuriôs, strictly speaking, 318,26;
322,26; 333,27; 336,26-7;
337,10-12; 343,30; **kurtos**, convex, 295,17; 347,12

lambanein, assume, 329,19
lexis, passage, 318,13-14
logos, formula, 340,20; 341,2-5;
argument, 292,22-293,8; 296,9;
297,19; 301,22; 302,26; 303,33;
306,27; 311,20; 324,10;
330,24.27; 333,11.13.32; 342,14;
347,10; 349,13; 351,20; 355,20;
360,13; 361,8.15; account, 314,13;
321,24.28; 323,27; 336,28
luesthai, be dissolved, 300,19-20;
312,11; 352,18; 353,6; 360,12

megethos, magnitude, 321,17-19
meros, part, 346,5; 347,21; 350,2;
355,31; 357,8
meson, middle, 313,29; 335,33; 346,7;
intermediate, 331,23-34; 332,15;
333,24.30; 334,2-4; 338,32; 340,31
metaballein, change, 301,35-302,28;
303,11.27; 305,20; 307,20;
308,33-309,26; 310,11.16; 311,31;
314,2; 316,17; 317,13-14; 341,26;
342,4-8.26; 343,20; 334,10-23;
357,25-9
metabolê, change, 294,21-2;
303,11-13.27; 304,26; 306,13;
307,25-7; 308,1.10; 309,29-33;
313,23-314,13; 315,30;
342,3.6.11; 343,8; 344,3-7; 354,26
metaxu, intermediate, 306,7;
332,9-21; 333,23-7; 336,4.5;
337,31; 338,19-25; 339,7.12;
340,25-34; 342,22; 344,4; 353,28
metekhein, participate, 306,23;
331,25; 333,32; 334,2; 336,5;
340,34; 341,18
methexis, participation, 361,10
morion, particle, 329,10-13
morphê, shape, 295,7; 307,19.25.30

Neikos, Strife, 293,20.22.26
noêtos, intelligible, 294,11; 296,18

opsis, sight, 321,29
osphrêsis, smell, 321,10
ouranos, heaven, 299,20-1; 300,3.9;
301,5; 303,18; 307,6; 312,9-28;
346,9-12; 357,13-14; 358,4;
358,32-359,1; 360,6.22.24
ousia, substance, 295,2-15;
296.11.15; 300,10; 301,13-16

pan, totality, 294,21-4; 296,3; 297,19,
paradeigma, exemplar, 301,17;
example, 311,22
paratasis, temporal extension,
313,19-31; extension, 314,3-9
peperasmenos, finite, limited, 301,5;
312,13; 341,24; 348,5-6;

Greek-English Index

348,11-13; 353,2-9; 360,6-18; 361,2.8-11
peras, limit, 296,25; 339,15-18; 339,30-340,11; 348,1; 358,19
periphora, circumference, 299,1
pheresthai, move, 295,10-11
Philos, Love, 293,20.25
phthartos, destructible, 292,15; 293,15-16; 297,1-298,7; 300,7-301,2; 303,13; 308,27; 310,27; 311,14-15; 316,13-317,16; 317,21-5; 319,7.12; 322,4-361,13; destroyed, 294,17.26; 307,18; 312,30; 322,14
phtheiresthai, be destroyed, 293,17-20; 294,28-9; 295,25-8; 296,2; 301,24; 303,1-2; 306,19; 307,15-308,20; 308,26; 309,13; 310,3.31.33; 311,12-30; 312,17-23; 316,16-317,1; 317,10-14
phthora, destruction, 294,25-295,27; 296,1; 306,4; 307,2.22.28.30; 308,4.15; 310,6.21; 312,24; 317,9-15; 318,23-4; 336,23; 343,23; 344,10-11; 357,26
phusikai arkhai, natural principles, 357,15-18
phusikon sôma, physical body, 312,24
phusikos, natural scientist, 304,15; 305,21; 306,6
phusis, nature, 295,1.12; 298,14-15; 301,3-6; 302,28; 303,2.22; 304,11; 305,17; 306,20-2; 307,4; 308,32; 330,22; 331,1; 333,2; 336,3; 339,5; 342,7; 351,20-353,28; 354,3-24; 357,2; 359,8-361,13
pistis, confirmation, 342,14; 353,19; 357,16
plêmmelês, irregular, 303,18-23.34
poiein, produce, 293,22-3
poiêtikon aition, ***poiêtikê aitia***, productive cause, 294,8; 299,23.29; 310,18
poiotês, quality, 357,25-9
pollakhôs legesthai, said in many ways, 312,31-313,13; 322,27
prosekhôs, directly, 344,20; 353,8; 358,32; 360,9.11.22; 361,9
protasis, proposition, 329,22; 332,28-33; 336,7
pseudos, false, 323,20-4; 324,6.20

pseudos, to, the false, 322,22-6; 323,29; 324,4-23; 325,5-8; 329,8
pur, fire, 294,4-5.21; 304,19; 342,10; 344,22; 354,28

sêmeion, point, 349,16
skhêma, figure, 295,7; 305,11; 321,16; 335,33; 361,4
skhêmatismos, configuration, 300,10
skopos, subject, 349,13
sôma, body, 295,16.22; 298,28; 300,4; 306,10.15; 308,19-20; 311,2; 312,22
sômatikos, corporeal, 296,12-15; 300,1-2; 303,22; 305,16-17; 311,31; 314,9; 352,32; 360,25-8
sômatoeidês, corporeal element, 307,3; 360,31-3; 361,15; corporeal in form, 312,10; 361,4
sophia, wisdom, 294,14
stoikheion, element, 293,23; 295,8; 302,7; 303,17; 304,6-7.17; 306,2-15; 307,26; 308,1-16; 344,11-26; 354,28; letter, 333,12; 339,9; 344,11-26; 345,15; 354,28; 361,1
summetros, commensurable, 323,11-15.33; 324,17-28; 330,14.16.29; 336,21; 337,2-3; 359,10
sumplokê, concatenation, 332,26-7
sunalêtheuien, be true at the same time, 328,28-329,8; 329,23; 334,11; 352,11
sunkrisis, putting together, 295,23
sunthetos, composite, 304,8.11.19.27; 305,11.22; 306,8; 342,11; 344,5.27; 355,15
sunuparkhein, obtain at the same time, 328,31; 329,27
sustasis, composition, 302,15; 308,19.31; 309,2-23; 310,22

taxis, order, 303,22; 305,10; 306,17.24; 311,30; ordering, 296,11; 304,2-5
telos, end, 298,33; 299,2; 307,1; 313,29; 346,4; 347,26; 354,15; limit, 320,28-321,15
theion sôma, divine body, 357,27
theios, divine, 360,3
theologos, theologian, 293,13; 294,8; 296,5.9.26

theos, God, 296,10; 298,15; 301,1.7; 312,12; 359,20-9; 360,18-29
tithenai, posit, 333,13; 334,34; 335,8; 345,31; 349,4; 352,12; 356,30
tropos, mode, 329,20-2; manner, 315,15.30.32; 316,9.18; 317,16

tukhê, luck, 354,10-21
zêtein, investigate, 297,18.22; 299,5; 310,9; 332,23; 334,16; 336,17; 337,16
zôion, animal, 307,7; 342,11.18

Subject Index

action, 65, 66, 71
  in time, 65, 66
actuality, 13, 51, 56, 69, 70, 74, 75
  priority of, 89 n. 89
air, 16, 17, 18, 108 n. 384
Alexander, 4
  and temporal beginning of the world, 7-12
  on Heraclitus, 5
  on Plato on the generation of the world, 7-12
  on perceptual capacity, 35
  on senses of 'destructible', 31-2
  on the capacity for change, 14
alteration, 5, 6, 17-18, 19-20, 77, 93 n. 150
Anaxagoras
  and hypothetical generation, 17
animals, 60-2, 81, 115 n. 501
Aristotle, *passim*
  Epitome of the *Timaeus*, 7
  On Generation and Corruption, 77
  On Meaning, 44, 102 n. 282
  Physics, 26, 65, 68, 77, 79, 95 n. 174, 110 n. 409, 111 n. 423
  Prior Analytics, 37, 39, 63, 98 n. 235, 99 nn. 245, 252, 108 n. 391
axiom, 51, 77

body
  and motion, 10-11, 79
  divine, 77
  limited, 79
  qualityless, 18
  simple, 61
  underlying, 20, 61

'capable', 32-6
capacity, 13-14, 21-5, 32-6, 97 nn. 222, 232
  defined by maximum, 33-6, 99 n. 246
  forward-looking, 59, 75, 76, 98 nn. 242-3, 101 n. 272, 107 n. 370, 113 n. 461
  for contraries, 38-40, 70-1, 74, 99 n. 247
  for eternal existence, 70-2
  for existence, 36-7, 42, 46-50, 54, 59, 61-2, 66-8, 69-70, 70-2, 73
  for non-existence, 41, 42, 43, 46-50, 50-2, 54, 66-8, 69-70, 70-2
  infinite, 36-7, 59, 68, 69, 100 n. 257, 260
  limited, 71-2
  preceded actualisation in time, 69-70
  time of, 36-7, 59-62, 68, 69-70, 99 n. 246
  see also potentiality
'Capacity Principle', 41, 57, 99 n. 252, 100 nn. 254, 257, 260, 265, 267, 101 n. 276, 104 n. 324, 106 n. 360, 110 nn. 415, 418
categories, 36
cause
  immobile, 72, 79; *see also* Prime Mover
  of existence, 73
  productive, 5, 10, 85 n. 25
chance, 73, 112 n. 454
change, 13, 18, 19-20, 21-2, 26-7
  eternal, 18
Christians, 84 n. 8, 86 n. 38, 87 n. 46, 90 n. 97, 92 n. 130
composites, 5, 16, 60, 62
composition, 21-2
contact, 26, 27, 30, 95 n. 188
contradiction, 44-5, 49, 50, 62, 71, 102 n. 294, 104 nn. 313, 320
  principle of non-, 44, 102 n. 283

Subject Index

contrariety, 44, 46-7, 47-9, 50, 57-8, 73, 102 n. 280, 103 nn. 305, 307, 106 nn. 364, 365
   and change, 77, 78
   definition of, 47-8, 102 n. 280
   'unmediated', 47-8, 103 n. 298

Demiurge, 18, 64, 72, 80
Democritus, 5
   and atoms, 6
   and 'generation', 6
   and infinity of worlds, 5-6, 22-3, 85 n. 19, 94 n. 151
   and void, 6
demonstration, 26, 51, 60, 64, 73, 76
'destructible', 25, 29-30, 33
   as proneness for destruction, 30, 32
   as suitability for destruction, 30, 96 n. 199
   at some time destroyed, 70-2, 78-9
   co-extensive with generable, 36-7, 40-1, 46-50, 50-2, 53-4, 54-60, 62-4, 77-8, 108 n. 388
   'of a nature to be destroyed', 70, 71, 73, 78
destruction, *passim*
   instantaneous, 29-30, 97 n. 212
   into contraries, 77
   temporal, 11, 36
diagonal, 33, 38, 39, 52-3
   incommensurability of, 33, 38, 39, 53, 78
diagrams, 15, 16
disorder, 80

earth, 16
elements, 4, 15, 16, 17, 18, 20, 60-2, 73, 80, 81, 91 n. 115, 108 n. 386
   corporeal, 80
   dissolved, 19-20
   'intermediate', 18, 90 n. 114
Empedocles, 4-5, 17, 19, 20
   generation as change, 17
   hypothetical generation, 17
   on Love and Strife, 4-5, 6, 20, 85 n. 28, 86 n. 36, 93 nn. 145, 148-9
   two worlds, 5, 22-3
eternal, the, 44
eternal persistence, 18, 43, 55-62, 99 n. 250
   incompatible with destructibility, 40-2, 43, 44-50, 50-2, 53-4
eternal things, 28, 31, 50-2

'even-odd', 47, 103 n. 302
evil, 80-1, 115 nn. 496, 500
   necessary if there is to be good, 81
excess and capacity, 36
exemplar, 12, 80 n. 83
existence,
   at a time, 40-50, 55-62

falsity, 37-9
   and deduction, 37, 98 nn. 235, 245
   hypothetical, 38-9, 41, 98 n. 239
   not always impossible, 39, 41
fire, 5, 16, 60, 62, 73
'for the most part', 73, 113 n. 456
form, 18, 20, 62, 80, 81, 91 n. 119, 108 n. 387, 115 n. 488
formula, 58

generable, *passim*
   entails destructible, 40-2, 46-50, 50-2, 53-4, 54-60, 62-4
'generated', 25, 28-9, 33
   cannot be indestructible, 64-8, 68-70, 72-4, 75
generation, *passim*
   and contrariety, 77, 109 n. 400
   and identity, 19-20
   from non-existent, 15, 22, 93 n. 138
   'hypothetical', 16-17, 18, 19
   instantaneous, 27, 28, 53, 95 nn. 183, 188
   mathematical, 16-17
   requires cause, 15
   temporal, 7-12, 14, 15, 16, 18
genus, 48, 103 n. 309
God, 11-12, 15, 79, 80-1, 82, 115 n. 500
   and evil, 80-1
   power of, 80-1

heaven, the, 10, 64, 79-80
   and God, 12, 79-80, 89 n. 80
   corporeality of, 10
   indissolubility of, 78
   limited, 89 n. 80
   motion of, 9-10, 11, 12, 79, 80
   ungenerated, 12, 77
Heraclitus, 4-5, 19
   and *ekpyrôsis*, 5, 85 n. 30
   and eternity of the world, 5
hypothesis, 13, 15, 16-17, 22, 41, 42, 51, 104 n. 324

Subject Index

'impossible', 27
impossibility, *see also* incapability
  for the ungenerable to be destroyed, 41-2, 57
  hypothetical, 37-9, 98 n. 236
  of actualised contradictories, 40, 43, 44, 66-7, 78
  of capacity for infinite existence and non-existence, 36-7, 97 n. 232
  unqualified, 37-9, 78
incapability, 27-8, 29, 31, 32-3
  defined by maximum, 34
'incapable', 32-6
'indestructible', 25-6, 29, 30-2, 33
  as not easily destroyed, 31, 32
  as not yet destroyed, 32
  entails ungenerable, 40-1, 46-50, 51-2, 54, 62-4, 108 n. 393
indestructibility
  inconsistent with generability, 11-12, 15-19, 36-7, 88 n. 78
  temporal, 11, 15-19, 88 nn. 75, 76, 78
induction, 12, 89, n. 87, 13
infinite regress, 26-7, 95 n. 174
infinity, 27, 36-40, 40-2, 109 n. 407
  and indeterminacy, 65-6
  definition of, 65, 109 n. 407
  no actualised, 110 n. 408
  'semi-bounded', 65, 73, 77-8, 106 n. 350, 107 n. 367, 108 nn. 382-3, 111 n. 428
  temporal, 64-5, 66-8, 68-70, 72-3, 113 n. 457
'intermediates', 46-8, 49-50, 55-60

lifting, 33-4, 35
luck, 73, 112 n. 454

man, by nature destructible, 81-2
matter, 18, 20, 21, 22, 60-2, 73, 74, 91 n. 119, 107 n. 381, 108 n. 387
  and identity-conditions, 19-20, 21, 60, 83 n. 8, 92 nn. 131-3, 108 n. 387
measure, 27
motion, 26-7
  eternal, 79, 80, 89 n. 80; *see also* heaven, the
  'of motion', 26-7

natural scientists, 17
nature, 73

corporeal 15, 17, 80
necessity,
  of existence, 48
  of the past, 75, 114 n. 468
negation, 44-50, 55-6, 57-8, 59, 72, 101 n. 278
Neoplatonists, 85, nn. 24-5
'nows', 67, 110 n. 413, 111 n. 426
  infinity of, 67

Philoponus, 84 n. 8, 86 n. 38, 87 n. 46, 90 n. 97
'physical arguments', 64, 76
plants, 60-2
Plato
  and argument, 4
  and disorderly elements, 14-15, 17, 18, 19, 90 n. 98
  and hypothetical generation, 16-17
  and the 'really real', 10, 11, 71, 88 n. 70
  and the world, 79-80; generated but indestructible, 7-12, 65-8, 70-2, 78; 'having its being in becoming', 8-9, 11, 17
  Laws, 34
  on time, 7, 9-10, 14
  Statesman, 15, 18-19, 80
  Theaetetus, 81
  Timaeus, 7-11, 15, 51, 64, 70, 109 n. 401
points, 68
possibility, *see* capacity, potentiality
  no impossibility results from, 99 n. 252; *see also* 'Capacity Principle'
potentiality, 56-7
  for opposing states, 39-40
  temporally prior to actuality, 13
  see also capacity, power
power, 79; *see also* capacity, potentiality
Prime Mover, 89 n. 80, 114 n. 485
principle, 16, 17
  natural, 76
Principle of Plenitude, 13, 89 n. 90, 92 nn. 136-7, 96 n. 199, 101 nn. 273, 276, 105 n. 327, 110 n. 415
Principle of Sufficient Reason, 90 n. 98, 110 n. 414, 112 n. 434
privation, 18, 19, 81, 91 n. 119
proof, *see* demonstration

quality, 36, 77

quantity, 36

reductio ad impossibile, 63

senses, 34-6
Stoics, 19
 and *ekpyrôsis*, 5
substance, 36
substrate, 61, 73, 76

theorem, 62
time
 and generation, 7-12, 15, 16
 and 'the now', 88 n. 65
 determinate, 55-7, 65
 of existence, 36-7, 55-60, 74-5
 infinity of, 22, 36-7, 41-2, 65, 66-8, 87 n. 44, 100 nn. 257, 260, 109 n. 407
 past, 7, 22
 pre-existence in, 16, 18, 56
 'tending towards infinity', 65
totality, the, 5, 8

'ungenerated', 25-8, 33
 and destructible, 64-5
 co-extensive with indestructible, 36, 50-2, 52-3, 62-4, 76

wasps, 61, 108 n. 385
water, 16, 17, 18, 60, 62, 108 n. 384

world, the, *passim*
 'capable of being otherwise disposed', 12-14
 dispositions of, 19-20
 eternity of, 19-20, 22, 36ff. *passim*
 'figurative' generation of, 7
 generated, according to other theorists, 4-5, 19-20, 21-2
 generated but indestructible, 19-20, 52, 70-2, 74
 generation from pre-existing elements, 13-14
 'hypothetical', 15-19
 identity-conditions of, 19-20, 21, 83 n. 8, 92 nn. 131-3
 indestructibility of, 3-4, 7, 74
 infinity of, 21-3
 intelligible, 5
 non-indestructibility of, 13-14, 40-2, 70-2
 non-recurrence of, 5-6
 perceptible, 5, 7, 71
 recurrence of, 13-14, 21-3, 93 n. 150, 94 nn. 151, 158
 temporal beginning of, 7-12, 13, 14, 15
 ungenerated, 3, 7, 42-3
 uniqueness of, 3

Xenocrates, 15, 90 n. 100
Xenophanes, 83 n. 7